ADVENTURES IN CONVERSATION

*Exercises in Achieving Oral Fluency
and Developing Vocabulary in English*

LYNNE HUNTER

CYNTHIA SWANSON HOFBAUER
*American Language Institute
San Diego State University*

PRENTICE HALL REGENTS, Englewood Cliffs, NJ 07632

Library of Congress Cataloging-in-Publication Data

HUNTER, LYNNE.
  Adventures in conversations: exercises in achieving oral fluency
and developing vocabulary in English/by Lynne Hunter and Cynthia
Swanson.

  ISBN 0-13-013921-1

  1. English language—Textbooks for foreign speakers.   2. English
language—Conversation and phrase books.   3. Vocabulary—Problems,
exercises, etc.   I. Swanson, Cynthia.   II. Title.
PE1128.H828   1989
428.3'4—dc19   88–39175
                                                                    CIP

Editorial/production supervision and interior design: TUNDE A. DEWEY
Cover design: WANDA LUBELSKA DESIGN
Manufacturing buyers: LAURA CROSSLAND/MIKE WOERNER

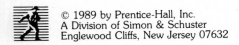
© 1989 by Prentice-Hall, Inc.
A Division of Simon & Schuster
Englewood Cliffs, New Jersey 07632

Printed in the United States of America
10 9 8 7 6 5 4 3 2 1

ISBN   0-13-013921-1

Prentice-Hall International (UK) Limited, *London*
Prentice-Hall of Australia Pty. Limited, *Sydney*
Prentice-Hall Canada Inc., *Toronto*
Prentice-Hall Hispanomericana, S.A., *Mexico*
Prentice-Hall of India Private Limited, *New Delhi*
Prentice-Hall of Japan, Inc., *Tokyo*
Simon & Schuster Asia Pte. Ltd., *Singapore*
Editora Prentice-Hall do Brasil, Ltda., *Rio de Janeiro*

To Our Parents

CONTENTS

Conversation Exercises

Chapter 9   ENTERTAINMENT   100

Vocabulary Exercises

Conversation Exercises

Chapter 10   THE WORLD   115

Vocabulary Exercises

Conversation Exercises

PREFACE

The most difficult aspect of teaching a conversation class is, almost certainly, motivating the students to speak. Too often, conversation classes fail because they rely on texts that emphasize topics in which students are not interested. Similarly, conversation books may frustrate students by asking them to discuss issues about which they are uninformed. Frequently, too, the exercises in conversation texts are so sketchily presented that the teacher lacks the time to do all the at-home preparation required to teach them successfully.

To sidestep the first of these drawbacks, a major goal in *Adventures in Conversation* has been to design exercises that are interesting. Much of the material, therefore, tends to the personal, the immediate, or the intriguing. In one instance, for example, students are asked to tell about an heirloom that they have received or may one day receive. Elsewhere, they are given the task of compiling a "book" of useful phrases for travelers. On still another occasion, their task is to write and act out a TV commercial.

To further ensure that the text will be interesting, a great diversity of conversation exercises have been included, for it was felt that variety in this area would be more inspiring than a predictable slate of activities.

A second objective of this text has been to provide students discussion topics that they know something about. Hence, in some instances, they are asked to share their values, tastes and preferences. In other cases, they may be asked to tell students from other cultures about their own.

A final goal has been to present the exercises in a form that would free the teacher from all but the most minimal at-home preparation. The completeness with which the exercises are set up in the student book, and the inclusion of examples and specific explanations for teaching the exercises in the *Teacher's Guide*, serve to accomplish this aim.

In summary, a great effort has been made to write a conversation text that will be stimulating, readily comprehensible to the students, and easy for the teacher to use. It is hoped that the latter will find *Adventures* a valuable aid in conducting that most challenging of all ESL courses to teach: the conversation class.

Acknowledgements

At Prentice Hall, we wish to thank Tina Carver, Editor-in-Chief; Anne Riddick, Editor; Andy Martin, Marketing Manager; Sylvia Moore, Managing Editor, and all of the others at Prentice Hall Regents who made this project possible.

We thank Gordon Johnson for encouraging us to begin this undertaking and Tunde Dewey, Production Editor, for her tireless and patient assistance with a seemingly endless project.

Same special thanks go to artist Ellen Sasaki for her imaginative and painstaking execution of the illustrations for this book. We would also like to extend our appreciation to Madeleine Scott for typing the first two drafts of the manuscript.

Finally, we wish to thank Betty Jurus and Nancy Painter of the *Writers' Bookstore and Haven* for their on-going encouragement and support.

TO THE TEACHER

This text is intended for intermediate learners of English as a second language. It provides at least enough material for a 15-week conversation class meeting 3 hours a week or a 10-week conversation class meeting 4 hours a week.

This book contains 10 chapters, grouped together roughly in terms or related subjects. Each of the chapters is divided into a vocabulary and a conversation section. The vocabulary section begins with a list of the new words to be taught in the chapter. Following this list are three vocabulary exercises, each of which reinforces a portion of the words just introduced. All the new vocabulary is utilized in the conversation exercises in the same chapter. The vocabulary from previous chapters is, moreover, recycled, wherever possible, in both the vocabulary and conversation exercises in chapters 2–10. (Although the chapters are not strictly arranged in order of difficulty, it is suggested that they be completed in sequence.)

Following the vocabulary exercises in each chapter are five conversation exercises. Their primary purpose is to get the students to speak English about a variety of subjects and to use the vocabulary in doing so.

The diversity of the exercises makes the text adaptable to a broad spectrum of students, allowing the teacher to focus upon those types of activities best suited to a particular class. The availability of such options encourages the instructor to adopt as flexible an approach as he or she deems fitting.

Most of the exercises have been designed so that they can be performed within class. There are a few exceptions, however. A handful of exercises may require that the students do some at-home preparation between the introduction of the activity and its performance in class.

It has been impossible to estimate the time that the exercises will take to perform. As every ESL instructor knows, each class progresses through activities at its own pace.

It is intended that *Adventures* be used with the *Teacher's Guide.* That guide contains detailed, specific instructions for presentation of the exercises, and should be of value even to the experienced conversation teacher.

Three general directions are sufficiently important to be mentioned here as well as in the *Teacher's Guide:* (1) instructions for presenting vocabulary exercises, (2) general directions for conversation exercises performed in groups, and (3) teacher correction techniques.

Instructions for Presenting Vocabulary Exercises

GENERAL COMMENTS

Twenty vocabulary words are introduced in each unit. The meaning of these words is then reinforced by three vocabulary exercises. These exercises are followed by five conversation exercises, which require the students to utilize the vocabulary words and their definitions.

Note: *Vocabulary words appear in boldface type in the conversation exercises of the chapter in which they have been introduced. When vocabulary words from previous chapters occur, either in vocabulary or in conversation exercises, they are italicized.*

VOCABULARY LISTS

Format   The vocabulary list at the beginning of each chapter is divided into various parts of speech and "Expressions." Under Expressions are grouped idioms, slang, and other vocabulary items that cannot strictly be classified as parts of speech.

GENERAL DIRECTIONS FOR USE OF THE VOCABULARY LISTS

Outside class   Before beginning each unit, have the students study the words and definitions for that unit at home. Tell them to be prepared to ask you questions regarding definitions of words they don't understand.

In class   Read over each word and definition as the students follow along in their books. Ask the students whether any of them have questions about the definition. If they do, expand the definition or provide an oral sentence example.

VOCABULARY EXERCISES

EXERCISE I.   **Read and Complete**
Have the students work in pairs to do this exercise. Encourage them to use contextual clues (clues from the rest of the sentence or dialogue) to help them guess the appropriate word to put into the blank. For each vocabulary word, you may also wish to introduce related words (other parts of speech from the same word family). Ask different pairs for their answers.

EXERCISE II.   **Listen and Choose**
In this exercise the students are asked to listen and choose the correct definition for each vocabulary word. Only one alternative is correct.

a.   Draw two stick figures on the board. Stand under the appropriate stick figure as you read each part of the dialogue to make students aware of the change in speaker. (Or ask one of the students to help you by playing one of the roles).

b.   Ask the students to close their books and listen as you read the complete dialogue aloud.

c.   Ask the students to open their books. Ask them to cover up the dialogue on the left-hand side of the page so that only the words and answer choices are visible. Begin rereading the dialogue, one part at a time. After each part, read the underlined vocabulary word and accompanying answer choices.

d.   Ask the students to choose the correct definition for each word.

e.   Ask different students for their answers.

EXERCISE III.   **Read and Describe**
Have the students read the story. Encourage them to ask questions about anything they don't understand. Then, have them work in pairs to describe each picture using the words beneath it. When the class has completed the exercise, call on a different student to describe each picture.

General Directions for Exercises Performed in Groups

In exercises that emphasize group consensus, each group should appoint a group leader, whose task it will be to maintain order in the group and make sure that all students participate. When the group's answers are to be presented before the class, each of the groups should also appoint a reporter to record the group's answers and a spokesperson to relate these answers to the class.

Teacher Correction Techniques

While the students are doing an activity, the teacher should circulate throughout the class to answer questions and facilitate. At the same time, he or she should make note of errors in grammar or vocabulary. At the end of the activity or class period, the teacher may wish to write the errors (one at a time) on the board, without reference to who made them. Then, he or she should ask the class what is wrong with the phrasing, and write the corrected version on the board.

TO THE STUDENT

Adventures in Conversation is designed to improve your vocabulary and conversational skills. After you have completed this book, you will know words that will help you talk about many different subjects. You will also feel comfortable speaking English about these topics in many different situations. This text will also help you learn about American culture and about the cultures of your classmates.

Adventures in Conversation is divided into ten chapters. Each chapter has two main sections: (1) vocabulary and (2) conversation.

At the beginning of each vocabularly section is a list of words. After you study this list, you will do three exercises that will help you remember the meanings of the words and give you practice in using them. You will continue to practice the vocabulary in the conversation exercises.

There are five conversation exercises in each chapter. They are not always the same. We have put many different kinds of conversation activities in this book to make learning English more interesting and enjoyable. So in some chapters, you will do role plays, solve problems, or tell other students about your country. In other chapters, you will describe pictures, talk about yourself, or make up stories.

Learning a language takes time, but it can be fun, too. It can be a way to understand other people and their cultures better. We hope that this is how learning English will be for you. We want it to be an adventure.

CHAPTER 1 Getting Acquainted

VOCABULARY

Study the following vocabulary.

Nouns

background – kind of family that someone comes from, his or her education, and the kinds of things that he or she has done

impression – ideas that people get about someone when they first meet him or her

nationality – national group that one belongs to

trait – special quality; a part of someone's personality (for example, kindness or a sense of humor)

Verbs

to affect – to cause a change in; to make an impression on

to experience – to feel (something) or have (something) happen to oneself

to initiate – to start or begin (something such as a conversation)

to introduce – to assist one person in meeting another for the first time

to recall – to remember

to recognize – to see and to know

to respect – to have a good opinion of

Adjectives

familiar – known or seen before

significant – important

similar – almost the same

sociable – friendly; liking to be with other people

Expressions

to be known for – to be famous for

to get acquainted – to get to know each other

to be used to – to be accustomed to, to be familiar with

to have (something) in common – to be like (someone) in some way; to be alike

small talk – light conversation; conversation about everyday, unimportant subjects

A Childhood in Singapore

With your partner, take turns reading lines of the following dialogue. Choose the correct vocabulary word to put into each blank.

(Mary Beth and her new friend, Eric, are sitting in a coffee shop. They are telling each other about themselves.)

ERIC: What do you think was the most _____ event in your life?

MARY BETH: Well, perhaps the thing that _____ me most was moving to Singapore with my parents when I was a child.

ERIC: That's something that most people never have a chance to

_____ . What was it like?

MARY BETH: I don't _____ the city very well because I was very young, but I do remember the people who lived there. They came from many different countries, and I soon learned to like and understand them.

ERIC: It's too bad that everyone doesn't have a chance to live in another

country. It might help them learn to _____ other people's ways of life.

experience – feel (something) or have (something) happen to oneself

affected – caused a change in; made an impression on

recall – remember

respect – have a good opinion of

significant – important

A Stranger in Rome

Cover the left-hand side of the page with a piece of paper. Then, listen as your teacher reads the dialogue. After each section, choose the best definition for the boldface word.

> (*Nick, an American, has just arrived in Rome. Marco, an Italian friend whom Nick met in San Francisco, has picked Nick up at the airport.*)

1. NICK: Do you have to drive so fast?
   MARCO: Everyone in my country drives fast. It's a national **trait.**

1. **trait** means:
   a. race
   b. quality
   c. thing that people never do

2.   NICK: Well, you never drove like this when we were in San Francisco.

MARCO: Sure I did. You've just forgotten. You'll get **used to** my driving again. But I'll slow down for now, if it'll make you feel better.

2.   **used to** means:
a. worried about
b. accustomed to
c. afraid of

3.   NICK: Thanks. Now I can get a better look at the city. (He looks out the window.) That's an interesting fountain.

MARCO: Yes. Rome is **known for** its fountains. It's also famous for many of its buildings and its statues.

3.   **known for** means:
a. famous for
b. unattractive because of
c. not famous for

4.   NICK: Well, it's a beautiful city. I'm sure glad I brought my camera.

MARCO: Yeah. There are lots of things to take pictures of here. But I hope you're not planning to spend all your time taking pictures. I have some friends who'd like to meet you. They've asked to be **introduced** to you.

4.   **introduced** to means:
a. assisted in meeting
b. remembered by
c. known by

5.   NICK: That's fine with me. I was hoping I'd get a chance to practice my Italian here.

MARCO: You will, although my friends will want to practice their English, too. If it's OK with you, I'll call them and ask them to meet us for lunch so the three of you can **get acquainted.**

5.   **get acquainted** means:
a. say goodbye to each other
b. get to know each other
c. leave each other

Making a New Friend

You or your partner should read the following story. Use the other words in the sentence to help you understand the boldface words.

Last summer my friend, Miriam, was in Athens. She was sitting in a sidewalk café, when she saw someone who looked **familiar.** At first she wasn't sure who he was. Then she **recognized** that he was a popular American rock star. Since she hadn't talked with another American for weeks, she was really happy to see someone of her own **nationality.** Miriam is shy and she sometimes has a hard time being **sociable,** but she went over and **initiated** a conversation with the rock star. She didn't ask him for his autograph, which is an American custom, because she didn't want to be impolite.

At first their conversation was just **small talk.** They talked about the weather and places they had visited in Greece. But soon they found out that they **had something in common** besides their nationality. They both had the same **background.** They had been born in Maryland and gone to college in Chicago. And they both liked sailing, photography, and **similar** types of music. Miriam must have made a good **impression,** because the next evening the rock star took her to a disco where his band was playing!

If you don't understand the meaning of the boldface words, review their definitions at the beginning of this chapter.

With your partner, use the words beneath each picture to describe it.

familiar

to recognize

nationality

background

to initiate

small talk

similar

impression

to have something in common

sociable

Note: New vocabulary words that are used in the chapter are in boldface; words that are in italics are vocabulary from earlier chapters.

CONVERSATION
Getting Acquainted

Follow along as the teacher reads the example and the questions formed from it. Ask the teacher for more examples if you do not understand how to form the questions.

Example: Find someone who likes the same hobby that you like.
Question 1: What hobby do you like?

or

Question 2: Do you like reading?

Now try to find students who **have something in common** *with you. Walk around the room and ask the other students questions based on the following list. Whenever you find a student who is* **similar** *to you, write his or her name on the line beneath the question that you have just asked.*

1. Find someone who likes the same kind of drink that you like.

   _____

2. Find someone who likes the same kind of dessert that you like.

   _____

3. Find someone who likes the same color that you like.

   _____

4. Find someone who likes the same kind of car that you like.

   _____

5. Find someone who likes the same kind of movies that you like (western,

   horror, love story). _____

   _____

6. Find someone who likes the same kind of music that you like.

   _____

7. Find someone who likes the same kind of animal that you like.

   _____

8. Find someone who likes the same famous person that you like.

   _____

9. Find someone who likes the same sport that you like.

   _____

10. Find someone who likes the same city that you like.

---

*Tell the class the name of another student who **has something in common** with you. Explain what the two of you **have in common**.*

A Bus Ride

*You are on a bus. **Initiate** a conversation with each person whom you sit next to. Begin by making **small talk** with the person. Ask questions like "How are you?", "Isn't the weather nice?", and "Do you have the time?" Find out what the person's **nationality** is. Ask the person about his or her **background** (where he or she went to school, what kind of work he or she does).*

Telling about Your Life

*With the other members of your group, look at the picture that your teacher chooses. Listen as he or she talks about the picture. Then, choose the picture that makes you think of something you have done or something you would like to **experience** in the future. Describe the picture to the group and tell in what ways it makes you think of how your life has been or how you would like it to be.*

Planning a Weekend

Part 1. *Your partner has just won a prize. The prize is a special weekend in a nearby city. Your partner will have a chance to meet a famous person and to do whatever he or she wants. Your job is to help plan the trip for your partner. Ask him or her the following questions. Circle his or her answers.*

1. Would you rather spend time
   (a) alone,
   (b) with a large number of friends and family members, or
   (c) with a close friend?

2. When you visit a new city, which of these things would you like to see the most?
   (a) art shows
   (b) zoos
   (c) amusement parks
   (d) museums

3. Would you rather
   (a) watch a sport or
   (b) play a sport yourself?

4. Do you prefer to play
   (a) individual or
   (b) team sports?

5. Do you prefer to watch
   (a) individual or
   (b) team sports?

6. Do you prefer to play sports
   (a) on dry land,
   (b) in the water, or
   (c) in the snow?

7. Do you prefer to watch
   (a) sports on dry land,
   (b) sports in the water, or
   (c) sports in the snow?

8. What kinds of movies do you like best?
   (a) movies that are scary
   (b) movies about love
   (c) movies about things that happen in the future
   (d) movies that are funny

9. What kind of music do you like best?
   (a) jazz
   (b) rock
   (c) classical music
   (d) music from your country

10. Which of these people would you probably **respect** and like to meet the most?
    (a) a famous scientist
    (b) a famous artist
    (c) a movie star
    (d) an important government leader

Reverse roles.

Part 2. *What would your partner like to do for his or her special weekend? Use the information from Part 1 to help you answer the following questions.*

1. Who would your partner like to spend his or her weekend with?
2. What things would your partner like to do?
3. What sports would your partner play or watch?
4. What other things would your partner do to relax?
5. What famous person would your partner like to be **introduced to?**

Tell each other about the weekends that you have planned for each other. Then tell each other if you like the weekend that was planned for you or not.

What Would You Do?

*Read Situations 1, 2, and 3 to your partner. After each situation is read, have your partner tell you what he or she would do in that situation. Listen carefully so that you can learn something about your partner. Then, tell him or her some good **traits** that you think he or she may have. Reverse roles for Situations 4, 5, and 6.*

Situation 1

You are at the home of your boss. He and his wife are **known for** being very clean and neat. Suddenly, you see someone whom you don't know spill coffee on the hostess' new rug. You see that this has been an accident, and you don't think that the person who spilled the coffee noticed it.

Situation 2

You arrive at a party. You don't **recognize** anyone there, but you'd like to make a good **impression.** You see a large group of smiling, laughing people, three people talking seriously, and one shy-looking person standing alone.

Situation 3

You are at an airport, and it is late at night. Your plane will not be leaving for another hour, and you are looking at an interesting magazine. A nice-looking stranger, who is very **sociable,** offers to buy you a cup of coffee.

Situation 4

You are sitting in an expensive restaurant and you see a woman come in alone. She looks **familiar,** and you think that maybe you've met her before, but you don't **recall** where and you're not sure who she is.

Situation 5

Your roommate comes home and tells you that she has just lost her job. Then she goes into her bedroom and closes the door. You see that this situation has **affected** her badly. She's **used to** going to work every day, and her job was very **significant** to her.

Situation 6

While you are shopping in a department store, you suddenly notice that you are no longer carrying a package that you had with you. You go back to the place where you think that you may have laid it down. Then you see someone walking away with a package that looks **similar** to yours.

CHAPTER
2 Holidays

VOCABULARY

Study the following vocabulary.

Nouns

costume – special clothing that a person wears to look like someone or something other than himself or herself

eve – the night or the whole day before a holiday

feast – large, special meal for many guests

festival – party that any person may attend and where people eat, drink, dance, and enjoy themselves

holiday basket – basket of food that is given to poor people on a holiday

ornament – decoration; thing used to make something else look pretty (for example, candles may be used as an ornament in the home)

parade – group of people dressed in costumes or playing musical instruments and walking or riding down a street as others watch

resolution – promise made to oneself that one will change something in one's life (for example, that one will stop smoking)

reunion – gathering of people (especially family members) who haven't seen each other for a long time

tradition – special custom, often one that is very old (for example, it is a tradition in many countries to give gifts to someone on his or her birthday)

Verbs

to celebrate – to pay attention to a holiday or special occasion by doing something special, such as having a party

to decorate – to add beautiful things to something to make it look prettier

to disguise – to dress in special clothing in order to look like someone or something other than oneself

to entertain – to see that one's guests have food, drink, and a good time

to exchange – to give each other (gifts)

to honor – to show one's high opinion of (someone or something)

to partake – to eat or drink something that is offered

to reminisce – to talk about experiences from the past

Adjectives

joyous – happy, glad

thankful – *experiencing* a feeling of thanks

A Happy Season

With your partner take turns reading lines of the following dialogue. Choose the correct vocabulary word to put into each blank.

(*Two friends, Fran and Gordon, are sitting in a restaurant near the ice rink. They are watching the skaters.*)

GORDON: I love December! It's such a _____ time of the year!

FRAN: That's true. It is a happy season. It's a time when families and old friends get together and _____ .

GORDON: I feel very _____ to have my family and friends.

FRAN: Me, too, and there's nothing that makes me happier than sitting down with them to eat a wonderful _____ .
Do you realize how many people don't have what we do?

GORDON: Yes, I do. And you know what I think we should do? I think that we should share what we have with others. Let's fill a

_____ and give it to a family that doesn't have enough to eat.

reminisce – talk about experiences from the past

holiday basket – basket of food given to poor people on a holiday

feast – large, special meal for many guests

joyous – happy, glad

thankful – *experiencing* a feeling of thanks

Getting Ready for Christmas

Cover the left-hand side of the page with a piece of paper. Then, listen as your teacher reads the dialogue. After each section is read, choose the best definition for the boldface word.

(It is the day before Christmas. Donna is sitting in her friend Julie's kitchen.)

1. DONNA: Oh dear! This is really terrible! Here it is the day before Christmas and I haven't even bought all my Christmas presents yet.

   JULIE: Well I haven't either. And the worst part is that so many stores close early on **Christmas Eve.**

1. **Christmas eve** means:
   a. the evening before Christmas
   b. the evening after Christmas
   c. Christmas day

2. DONNA: Oh no! I forgot about that. Now I suppose I'll have to do my shopping at the twenty-four-hour drugstore.

   JULIE: What about the Christmas **festival** you were going to? I'm surprised you didn't buy some gifts there. . . . Or did you just spend all your time dancing and eating?

2. **festival** means:
   a. play
   b. holiday dinner at someone's home
   c. public party at which there are refreshments, dancing, and games

3. DONNA: I didn't go to it. I was supposed to make cookies to sell there, and I didn't have time. It was really embarrassing.

   JULIE: That's too bad. I guess we'd better do our shopping. And not only do I have to buy gifts, but I still need to buy more **ornaments** to hang on my Christmas tree. I saw some really pretty ones in a department store, but I don't know if they're still there.

3. **ornaments** means:
   a. paper used to wrap Christmas presents
   b. pretty things used to make something beautiful
   c. Christmas toys

4. DONNA: Aah! I'm getting nervous! When are we going to get time to relax?

   JULIE: Not today. I've still got lots of shopping to do. Everyone I know seems to want to **exchange** gifts this year.

4. **exchange** means:
   a. to give each other
   b. to wrap
   c. to make

5. DONNA: I hate to say this, but I'll be glad when the holidays are over. Next year I'm going to start getting ready a lot earlier.

   JULIE: I'll believe that when I see it. That's the promise I make to myself every year, but it's a **resolution** I never keep.

5. **resolution**
   means:
   a. promise made by a person to him- or her-self
   b. promise made to a friend
   c. promise made to a stranger

American Holidays

You or your partner should read the following story. Use the other words in the sentence to help you understand the boldface words.

Americans love holidays. Most people's favorite holiday is probably Christmas. People enjoy Christmas **traditions,** such as **decorating** the Christmas tree with lights and ornaments or singing Christmas songs. Many people like to hold parties to **entertain** their friends, and everyone likes to **partake** of special Christmas foods and drinks, such as plum pudding and eggnog.

For many people, the best part of Christmas is family **reunions.** Often, family members travel thousands of miles to be together at this season.

Another holiday that people enjoy **celebrating** is Halloween. Halloween is very different from Christmas. One of the reasons that it is so popular is that both adults and children enjoy **disguising** themselves in **costumes.** They like to look like someone different on this day. Of course, adults don't go to their neighbors' houses to ask for candy, as children do. They go to parties instead.

Some holidays aren't so much fun. One of these is President's Day. This day **honors** two American presidents. Not much happens on President's Day, although there are special **parades** with marching bands and people riding in cars covered with flowers. But people get to stay home from work on President's Day. So it is better than having no holiday at all.

If you don't understand the meaning of the boldface words, review their definitions at the beginning of this chapter.

With your partner, use the words beneath each picture to describe it.

to honor

parade

reunion

tradition

to celebrate

to decorate

to disguise

costume

to partake

to entertain

CONVERSATION
Greeting Cards

The verses for the greeting cards beneath each picture are out of order. With your partner, put the lines in order. Use the picture above each verse to help you. Write your answers on the lines.

And have much cause to **celebrate,**
Or eat a turkey leg, at least,
Here's hoping you will have a **feast**
And be **thankful** on this autumn date.

_____

_____

_____

_____

_____

_____

Happy Thanksgiving! _____

That you, your family and your friends
To you, the best of everything
I hope the next twelve months will bring
Would like to have when this year ends.

_____

_____

_____

_____

_____

_____

Happy New Year! _____

And chocolate candy, too,
And that is: I love you.
I could send a heart, a ring,
But I can only say one thing,

Happy Valentine's Day!

To go and put our **costumes** on!
See black cats hiding from the light
They tell us that the time has come
And pumpkins smiling in the night?

Happy Halloween!

Good friends with whom to **reminisce**.
And share love with your family,
Be **joyous** as you trim the tree,
And may the season bring you this:

Merry Christmas!

A Holiday in Your Country

What is a holiday in your country? Tell the other group members:

1. what the name of the holiday in your country is.
2. when the holiday is.
3. what the holiday **honors.**
4. what activities are popular on this holiday.
5. whether people **disguise** themselves in **costumes** on this holiday, and if so, what kinds of **costumes** they wear.
6. what kinds of presents people **exchange** on this holiday.
7. whether people make **resolutions** on this holiday, and, if so, what kinds of **resolutions** they make.
8. whether people **partake** of special foods and drinks on this holiday.
9. whether people give **holiday baskets** on this holiday.
10. how popular family **reunions** are on this holiday.

Holiday Traditions around the World

*What is an activity that is a **tradition** on a holiday in your country (for example, breaking a piñata—Mexico, fighting with kites—Japan, hanging stockings on Christmas Eve—Great Britain and the United States)? Tell the other group members how this activity is done.*

A Holiday Gift

What was the favorite gift that you received on a holiday (or that you would like to receive)? Tell your partner:

1. what the gift was.
2. what it looked like.
3. who made it (a person, a company, etc.).
4. what country it came from.
5. what it was used for.
6. what holiday you received it on.
7. who gave it to you.
8. why you like it so much.
9. what happened to it.

Answer any questions that your partner asks you about your gift. Then, have your partner tell you about his or her favorite holiday gift.

Plan a Festival

With your partner, choose one of the following themes for a holiday:

1. a day to **honor** friendship
2. a day to **honor** animals
3. a day to **honor** people from other countries
4. a day to **honor** the city you live in
5. a day to **honor** children
6. a day to **honor** health
7. a day to **honor** books
8. a day to **honor** art

(*If you do not like any of these themes, you and your partner may choose one of your own.*)

*Plan a **festival** for the holiday that you have chosen. Talk about:*

1. what foods you would serve.
2. what drinks you would serve.
3. how you would **decorate** the place that was used for the **festival**.
4. the **costumes** that people would wear.
5. the activities that would be offered to **entertain** people (such as a **parade**).
6. the gifts that people would give each other.

*Tell the class about your holiday and its **festival**.*

CHAPTER

3 Home

Vocabulary

Study the following vocabulary.

Nouns

downpayment – the first payment that one makes when he or she is buying a house

dwelling – apartment, house, or other building where people live

furnishings – furniture, rugs, and other things used to *decorate* a house

house rules – rules that the owner or manager asks a tenant to obey

landlady – woman who owns houses or apartments and rents them to others

landlord – man who owns houses or apartments and rents them to others

maintenance – care of a house or apartment to keep it in good condition

rental agreement – paper that a tenant must sign; it tells such things as the amount of money to be paid for renting a house or apartment

security deposit – payment that the owner may keep if something is broken by the tenant

tenant – person who lives in a rented house or apartment

vicinity – particular area or neighborhood

Verbs

to be situated – to be located

to evict – to make (someone) move out of a rented house or apartment

to lease – to agree to rent a house or apartment for a certain period of time

to remodel – to change (a house) by making the rooms different or adding new rooms

to reside – to live (at or in a place)

Adjectives

cozy – warm and comfortable

occupied – having someone in it

spacious – roomy; having a lot of room

vacant – empty; having no one in it

A New Tenant

With your partner, take turns reading lines of the following dialogue. Choose the correct vocabulary word to put into each blank.

(*Mrs. Frazier, an older woman, is talking to Margaret, a young woman who wants to rent one of her apartments.*)

MRS. FRAZIER: I hope you'll like living in my apartment building. The last

_____ did. He was here for three years.

MARGARET: I'm sure I will. You know, I've been looking for a place to
                   live for a long time. All the other apartments in the area seem

                   to be _____ .

MRS. FRAZIER: Yes, well, this building is usually full, too. In fact, your apart-

                   ment has been _____ only since this
                   morning.

MARGARET: Well, I'm glad to have found it. And I'm glad you live here

                   in the building, too. My last _____ lived
                   in another part of town, and she didn't like having to drive
                   over to my apartment whenever there was a problem.

MRS. FRAZIER: I know what you mean. Well, here is the

                   _____ to sign. It just says that you must
                   pay $450 on the first of the month and that you'll let me know
                   thirty days before you move. I think you'll be very happy here.

rental agreement – paper that a tenant must sign

tenant – person who lives in a rented house or apartment

vacant – empty; having no one in it

occupied – having someone in them

landlady – woman who owns houses or apartments and rents them to others

Against the House Rules

Cover the left-hand side of the page with a piece of paper. Then, listen as your teacher reads the dialogue. After each section is read, choose the best definition for the boldface word.

(*Kevin has just come out of his history class at the university. He sees his friend, Laurie, in the hall.*)

1. KEVIN: Hi, Laurie. How do you like your new apartment?

    LAURIE: Really well. It's in an old house that was built in 1890. The owner **remodeled** it recently by adding another bedroom.

    1. **remodeled** means:
        a. tore (it) down
        b. built (it)
        c. made (it) different by changing or adding rooms

2. KEVIN: What's the owner like?

    LAURIE: Well, he seems nice. But it's hard to tell about **landlords.** They always seem nice at first.

    2. **landlords** means:
        a. neighbors
        b. women who own houses or apartments
        c. men who own houses or apartments and rent them to others

3. KEVIN: Do you have to pay a lot for the apartment?

    LAURIE: No, but I had to pay $300 as a **security deposit** in case I break something.

    3. **security deposit** means:
        a. money given to the police to keep a home safe
        b. money that an owner pays for home insurance
        c. money given to an owner to keep if something is broken

4. KEVIN: That's a lot of money. But I doubt if you'll break anything. Do you think you'll be in the apartment for a long time?

    4. **lease** means:
        a. move out of
        b. rent (a house

LAURIE: Probably. I plan to **lease** it for the next
                three years, until I finish school.

                                    or apart-
                                                    ment) for a
                                                    certain pe-
                                                    riod of time
                                                c. put furniture
                                                    into

5.   KEVIN: Well, your apartment sounds great. Why
                don't you have a party and invite your
                friends over?
      LAURIE: Sorry, Kevin. I can't have parties there.
                They're against the **house rules.**

5. **house rules**
    means:
    a. rules that
        someone
        renting a
        house or
        apartment
        must obey
    b. rules that
        someone liv-
        ing in a
        house or
        apartment
        makes his or
        her guests
        obey
    c. state laws
        about who
        can live
        where

Where Americans Live

You or your partner should read the following story. Use the other words in the sentence to help you understand the boldface words.

In the United States, many people once lived in large two- and three-story homes. Today many people would like to live in such **dwellings,** but most people can't. They don't have enough money to buy them or even to make the first **downpayment.** So, many people rent from month to month.

But some Americans really want to live in a house of their own. So they build their own home or they buy a house that is **situated** in a **vicinity** where homes are cheaper. It is better to **reside** in a bad part of town, they think, than not to live in a house at all. Or they buy an old house and remodel it. Then they *decorate* it with antique **furnishings.** Sometimes, they can make an old house look more beautiful than a new one.

Usually, it is not difficult for people to find an old home to buy. Many older people decide that they don't need a **spacious** home after their children leave. So they sell their house and move to a **cozy** apartment.

But when people move into a house, they sometimes have problems. Home-owners have to do their own **maintenance.** For example, if there is a problem with the plumbing, one can't ask the landlord or landlady to fix it. On the other hand, people can remodel their homes in any way they want without having to be afraid of being **evicted** by the owner. Overall, most Americans would probably prefer to live in a house rather than in an apartment.

If you don't understand the meaning of the boldface words, review their definitions at the beginning of this chapter.

With your partner, use the words beneath each picture to describe it.

downpayment

cozy

to evict

dwelling

furnishings

vicinity

to reside

spacious

maintenance

to be situated

CONVERSATION
Calling a Repairperson

Part 1. *Read the dialogue that the teacher assigns you with your partner, and try to learn it so that you can say it with your book closed.*

The Broken Window

MR. STONE: I'd like to speak to Mr. Johnson, please.

MR. JOHNSON: This is Mr. Johnson.

MR. STONE: Oh, hello. This is Eric Stone. My living room window was broken this afternoon. Can you repair it?

MR. JOHNSON: Sure. I can come over tomorrow afternoon. Is that OK?

MR. STONE: Yes. You charge about $100, don't you?

MR. JOHNSON: Usually, if it's a small window. Say, didn't I repair a window for you a few weeks ago?

MR. STONE: Yes, you did.

MR. JOHNSON: Oh, and your children have broken the window again? Were they playing ball in the house?

MR. STONE: Well, no, I told them not to do that anymore. This time *I* broke it. I was practicing my golf swing.

An Embarrassing Mistake

MS. HARRIS: Harris's TV repair.

MS. JONES: Hello. I was wondering whether you could help me. I have a problem with my TV.

MS. HARRIS: What kind of problem?

MS. JONES: Well, I turned it on this afternoon, and nothing happened.

MS. HARRIS: OK. I'll come over and take a look at it in a little while.

MS. JONES: How much do you charge?

MS. HARRIS: Twenty-five dollars an hour.
MS. JONES: All right. My name is Mary Jones, and I live at 3501 Ivy Street.
MS. HARRIS: OK, Ms. Jones. See you soon.
MS. JONES: Wait, Ms. Harris! Oh, I'm so embarrassed. I just noticed that the TV isn't plugged in.

The Lost Ring

MS. CARSON: Hello, is this Mr. Jackson, the plumber?
MR. JACKSON: Yes. What can I do for you?
MS. CARSON: I've dropped a ring down the sink, and I can't get it out. Do you think that you can?
MR. JACKSON: I may be able to.
MS. CARSON: Can you come over now? I've had the ring for years, and I'd hate to lose it.
MR. JACKSON: I guess so. What's your address?
MS. CARSON: 7170 Woodmere Road. And my name is Samantha Carson.
MR. JACKSON: Well, don't worry, Ms. Carson. My shop's in your **vicinity**, so I can be there in a few minutes.

Present your dialogue to the class.

Part 2. *With your partner, make up a dialogue like one of the dialogues in Part 1. Then write it down, and try to learn it so that you can say it with your book closed.*

A: _____

B: _____

A: _____

B: _____

A: _____

B: _____

A: _____

B: _____

Present the dialogue to the class.

Shopping for a Home

*You and your partner are each looking for a home to buy. You have saved enough money to make a **downpayment** on any one of the six homes in the pictures. Ask your partner the following questions:*

1. Which **dwelling** would you most like to live in? Why?

2. What do you like best about this house? (That it's modern, that it's old, that it has two stories, for example.)

3. Is there anything about the house that you have chosen that you would like to change?

4. Where would you like the house to be **situated**? Why?

5. Who would you like to be living in the house with?

Reverse roles.

Buying Furnishings for a New Home

*You and your partner have just bought a **spacious** new home in San Francisco. You have $10,000 that the two of you can spend for **furnishings.** By yourself, look at the following list and decide what you would like to buy. Together, discuss what each of you has chosen and come to an agreement about what you will buy.*

1. _____ Limoges dishes ($1,000)
2. _____ exercise equipment ($1,500)
3. _____ dishes made of plastic ($50)
4. _____ big-screen TV ($1,500)
5. _____ modern leather sofa and chairs ($3,000)
6. _____ antique crystal chandelier ($2,000)
7. _____ bed and dressers made of rosewood ($3,500)
8. _____ microwave oven ($200)
9. _____ painting by Monet ($1,500)
10. _____ waterbed ($300)
11. _____ stereo ($1,000)
12. _____ traditional velvet-covered sofa and chairs ($5,000)
13. _____ antique Chinese vase ($8,000)
14. _____ jacuzzi ($3,000)
15. _____ set of the greatest books ever written bound in leather ($1,250)
16. _____ sauna ($1,500)

17. _____ gas fireplace ($1,000)

18. _____ aquarium ($300)

19. _____ dishwasher ($500)

20. _____ video cassette player ($1,000)

Making House Rules

How would you solve the problems that these people might have if they lived together? With the other two or three group members, decide which roommate you want to be. Then read the description of yourself to the other members of your group.

Roommates

Kevin

- is afraid of having his possessions stolen
- is very clean and neat
- *is used to* watching TV until late at night
- smokes

Scott

- has a dog
- doesn't like to wash dishes
- studies hard and has to get up early
- plays classical music on the stereo

Todd

- has many noisy friends
- doesn't always remember to lock the doors
- doesn't like smoking
- doesn't like classical music

Dale

- doesn't like dogs
- sometimes leaves clothes on the bathroom floor
- owns the only TV in the house (it is in Dale's bedroom)
- doesn't like a lot of visitors

List the problems that you might have if you lived together.

Problem 1: _____

Problem 2: _____

Problem 3: _____

Problem 4: _____

Problem 5: _____

Problem 6: _____

*What **house rules** would you make to help solve these problems?*

House Rules

Noise: _____

_____

Visitors: _____

_____

TV: _____

_____

Locking windows and doors: _____

_____

Housework: _____

_____

Smoking: _____

_____

Tell the class the problems you might have if you lived together and the house rules that you would make to solve them.

Living in the City

With your partner(s), act out a role play.

Situation 1

Mrs. O'Hara: Your **tenant's** children are still playing baseball in your yard. They broke one of your windows once. You are afraid that another window will be broken. You are also afraid that one of your children will be hit by the ball. You have already asked the children to stop, but they won't. You are thinking of **evicting** your **tenant.** You explain the problem to her and tell her how you feel about it.

Annette: Your children love to play baseball. They play in your **landlady's** yard because your yard is too small. It's true that they broke her window, but you paid for it, so she shouldn't be worried. You listen to your **landlady** and tell her why your children play in her yard and what you plan to do.

Situation 2

Diane: Your next-door neighbor's son has a new set of drums. He plays them day and night. You can hear him even when your windows are closed. You would like to be able to read or listen to music. And you are very tired because you can't get any sleep. No one else is complaining, because the house on the other side of your neighbor is not **occupied.**

Ron: Your son washed dishes in a restaurant to earn money to buy drums. He has played the piano since he was a child, but the musical instrument that he's always wanted to play the most is the drums. He was so happy when he bought some for himself that you would feel bad if you asked him not to play them.

Situation 3

Mary: While you are watching TV late one night, you hear a knock at the door. Usually, you feel safe living in your **cozy** little house, but tonight you feel afraid because the houses on both sides of you have just become **vacant**. You **reside** in a big city and there have been some problems in your part of town. You look out the window and see two men whom you don't *recognize* standing at the door. You never open the door to strangers. You talk to these men through the window and decide what to do.

Ted: Your car has broken down a block away, so you need to use someone's phone to call your brother, Don. There is only one house with lights on on this street, and there are no phone booths nearby. You tell this woman what has happened and ask her to help you.

Tim: You and Ted are on your way home from a camping trip. You're both very tired and it's cold outside. You hope that this woman will let Ted use her phone so that he can call his brother. You know that she is afraid to let you in, so you say things to her that will make her less afraid.

Situation 4

Linda: You know that the carpet was already torn when you moved into your apartment. Your **rental agreement** says that your **landlord** is supposed to do **maintenance** here, so you go to your **landlord** and tell him about the problem. You feel unhappy that you **leased** this apartment.

Aaron: You have just **remodeled** this apartment. You put a new carpet in, so you don't see how the carpet could be torn. You think your **tenant** tore the carpet and that she should pay for it. Maybe you will use her **security deposit** for this purpose.

CHAPTER
4 Food

VOCABULARY

Study the following vocabulary.

Nouns

appetite – desire to eat

cuisine – style of cooking (such as French cuisine or Japanese cuisine)

etiquette – manners; way of behaving

gourmet – someone who is knowledgeable about food and drink

ingredient – something that is mixed with other things to prepare a food

recipe – instructions for preparing something to eat or drink

silverware – metal forks, knives, and spoons

snack – small amount of food eaten between meals

utensil – tool used for cooking, such as a measuring cup

vegetarian – person who does not eat meat

Verbs

to clear (the table) – to remove dishes and silverware from the table after a meal

to set (the table) – to put dishes and silverware on the table before a meal

to taste – to have a certain flavor (for example, sugar tastes sweet)

Adjectives

appetizing – appearing or smelling good to eat and having a good flavor

exotic – foreign; interesting and different

nutritious – filled with vitamins and other substances that are good for the body

scrumptious – delicious, wonderful to eat

starved – very hungry

Adverb

heartily – with a lot of energy and with great interest (for example, someone eats heartily when she or he is hungry)

Expression

junk food – food that isn't good for the health and that is usually high in calories (for example, potato chips)

A Picnic Lunch

With your partner, take turns reading lines of the following dialogue. Choose the correct vocabulary word to put into each blank.

(*It is a beautiful sunny day. Nick and Jean, two friends, are planning to have a picnic lunch in the park.*)

NICK: Let's open up our picnic lunch! I'm _____!

JEAN: Well, you'll be happy. I haven't exactly made a

_____; I've prepared a lot of food!

NICK: Great! I'm glad you thought about my _____.

JEAN: Oh, no! I've forgotten the _____!

NICK: That doesn't matter! We'll eat without it. Who cares about

_____ at a picnic!

silverware – metal forks, knives, and spoons

etiquette – manners; ways of behaving

snack – small amount of food eaten between meals

appetite – desire to eat

starved – very hungry

A Nutritious Meal

Cover the left-hand side of the page with a piece of paper. Then, listen as your teacher reads the dialogue. After each section is read, choose the best definition for the boldface word.

(Mary is visiting her sister, Lisa. Mary is in the living room. Suddenly, Lisa calls to her from the kitchen.)

1. LISA: I'm getting ready to cook dinner. What do you feel like eating?

    MARY: I don't know. What do you think would **taste** good?

2. LISA: Oh, maybe some hamburgers and french fries.

    MARY: Really? I've been eating a lot of things that aren't good for me lately. How about something **nutritious** like eggplant casserole?

1. **taste** means:
   a. look
   b. smell
   c. have a certain flavor

2. **nutritious** means:
   a. filled with things that are good for the body

b. filled with things that are bad for the body

c. filled with things that make the body weak

3. LISA: OK. How do I make it?

    MARY: Don't you have a cookbook? The **recipe** should be in it.

3. **recipe** means:
   a. cookbook
   b. foods that are used to cook something
   c. instructions for cooking something

4. LISA: Well, it isn't in any of the cookbooks I have. Maybe you can tell me how to make it.

    MARY: OK. First, make sure you have the **ingredients.** You'll need some eggplant, of course, and then three tomatoes . . . or is it four squash?

4. **ingredients** means:
   a. pans that are used to cook with
   b. instructions for cooking something
   c. foods that are mixed with other foods in cooking

5. LISA: Come on! How can I make something if you can't even tell me what to put in it?

    MARY: You're right. Never mind. I was in the mood for **junk food,** anyway. I'll go buy some potato chips and soda while you're making the hamburgers.

5. **junk food** means:
   a. food that is bad for the health
   b. food that is good for the health
   c. food that is very expensive

American Eating Habits

You or your partner should read the following story. Use the other words in the sentence to help you understand the boldface words.

Many foreign people think that Americans usually eat hamburgers. But the truth is that many people in the US have become **vegetarians,** who eat little or no meat. Most Americans, however, like many different kinds of foods. They especially love **exotic** foods, and restaurants that serve French, Arabic, Mexican, Japanese, Chinese, and African **cuisine** are among their favorites.

Americans also love to cook. And they don't always make simple things. Some of them are real **gourmets,** and they enjoy preparing fine meals. They spend thousands of dollars each year on cookbooks and cooking **utensils** to use in their kitchens. Like people in many countries, people in the US love to *entertain,* so they often invite people to dinner.

When the guests arrive, they find a table beautifully **set** with candles and fine china, because a meal is more **appetizing** when it is served in pleasant surroundings. When guests sit down to eat, they eat **heartily,** and when it is time to **clear** the table, they feel good. For many Americans, food that is cooked at home is the most **scrumptious** of all.

If you don't understand the meaning of the boldface words, review their definitions at the beginning of this chapter.

With your partner, use the words beneath each picture to describe it.

gourmet

to clear

scrumptious

exotic

cuisine

heartily

vegetarian

appetizing

to set

utensil

CONVERSATION
American Table Manners

*With the other members of your group, name the **eleven** things in each picture that you think might be considered bad **etiquette** in the United States. Write down your answers.*

In a Restaurant

1. _____

2. _____

3. _____

4. _____

5. _____

6. _____

7. _____

8. _____

9. _____

10. _____

11. _____

In a Home

1. _____

2. _____

3. _____

4. _____

5. _____

6. _____

7. _____

8. _____

9. _____

10. _____

11. _____

Tell the class what's wrong in each picture.

Table Manners in Your Country

*What things are considered bad **etiquette** in your country? With the other members of your group, take turns reading the following questions. After each question is read, every group member should answer about his or her country.*

1. What things shouldn't people bring to the table? (For example, in the United States, it is bad manners to bring a book to the table.)

2. What things shouldn't people wear at the table? (For example, in the United States, it is bad manners for men to wear a hat at the table.)

3. What things shouldn't people say during a meal? (For example, in the United States, it is bad manners to say, "This food doesn't look very **appetizing.**")

4. What shouldn't people do with their napkins? (For example, in the United States, it is bad manners for people to wear their napkins around their necks.)

5. What shouldn't people do with their **silverware,** if **silverware** is used in your country? (For example, in the United States, it is bad manners for people to dip their own forks and spoons into the serving dishes.)

6. What shouldn't people do with their dishes? (For example, in the United States, it is bad manners for people to lift their dishes up to their mouths.)

7. What shouldn't people do with their body? (For example, in the United States, it is bad manners for people to put their elbows on the table while they are eating.)

8. How shouldn't people behave toward others at the table? (For example, in the United States, it is bad manners for people to begin eating before others have been served.)

Tell the class about something that you learned about another country from a group member.

What to Eat or Drink?

You and your partner have just become roommates. You need to make some decisions about the following situations. By yourself, decide what you should do in each situation. Then, discuss the decisions that you and your roommate have made, and come to an agreement about what you should do about each situation.

Situation 1

The doorbell rings. There is someone at the door who wants to sell you bottled water. Bottled water is good for the health, but it is more expensive than regular water. What do you do?

Situation 2

You are **starved,** but you are both too tired to prepare a meal. So you decide to eat out. There are two restaurants in the *vicinity*: one serves fast food that is very greasy, and the other serves health food, but it is expensive. What do you do?

Situation 3

You are going to have a party, and you need to decide what kind of **snacks** you will serve. You are both **vegetarians,** but your friends aren't. They like **junk food.** You must choose between foods such as cookies and chips, and **nutritious** foods such as vegetables and fruits. What do you do?

Situation 4

You are shopping together in a grocery store, and you see some bread for sale. It is several days old, but it is being sold at half-price. What do you do?

Situation 5

You've just moved into a neighborhood, and you need to decide where to do your shopping. You can either go to a store that sells health food or to a regular grocery store. The food at the health food store costs more. What do you do?

Uncomfortable Situations

With your partner(s), act out a role play.

Situation 1

Husband: You are eating dinner with your wife at a *cozy* restaurant that serves **exotic cuisine.** You are surprised when she finds a fly in her soup. You don't think that you should pay for your wife's meal, or your own meal, either.

Wife: When you find a fly in your soup, you lose your **appetite.** You now think that the restaurant isn't as clean as you thought it was. The restaurant is a very expensive one, and it is filled with people. You don't care whether they hear what you say to the waiter.

Waiter: You have been a waiter here for many years. You are proud to work at such a fine restaurant. No one has ever found a fly in his or her food before tonight. You try to make the customers be quiet so that they won't tell the other people in the restaurant about what has happened. You think that the husband should pay for his meal, even if the wife doesn't pay for hers.

Situation 2

Customer: You get some milk from your refrigerator and discover that it is bad. Since you just got it yesterday, you think it must have been bad when you bought it. You take it back to the store and ask for your money back. You know that the clerk remembers selling you the milk, and you think that he's just trying to find a way not to return your money.

Clerk: You don't remember the customer who asks for his money back. You're not sure that he even bought the milk in this store. (He doesn't have a receipt.) Also, you're not sure the milk is bad. You don't want to give the customer his money back.

Situation 3

Wife: You are a bit of a **gourmet** and just to please you, your husband has been taking classes to become an excellent cook. Yesterday, he found a special **recipe** in a cookbook and spent hours making dinner for you. He expects you to eat **heartily.** But when you start to eat, you find that the food doesn't **taste** very good. You get a strange look on your face at first, but you try to hide it. You don't want your husband to feel bad. You eat a few bites of the food and then tell your husband that you are full.

Husband: You have spent all day cooking a meal for your wife. You spent a lot of money for the **ingredients** and you even had to buy special cooking **utensils** to make the meal. You're happy to serve your wife the dinner, but when she begins to eat, you see a strange look on her face. You think that maybe she doesn't like the food you've made.

Planning a Dinner

Part 1. *What kind of a meal would you serve a foreign guest? Ask your partner the following questions. Write down his or her answers.*

1. What kinds of things do people from your country like to eat?
2. What kinds of things do people from your country like to drink?
3. Are there any foods or drinks that are not served in your country?
4. In your country, what room in the home is used for eating?
5. What kinds of *furnishings* do you have in this room?
6. What do people use when they **set** the table?
7. At what time do people in your country **set** the table and at what time do they **clear** the table after the evening meal?

Reverse roles.

Part 2. *Plan a dinner for each other. The dinner that each of you plans should be **similar** to one that would be served in your partner's country. Use the information from Part 1 to help you answer the following questions.*

1. What time would you serve the meal?
2. What kinds of food would you serve?
3. What kinds of drinks would you serve?
4. Where would you serve the meal (which room)?
5. What kind of seating arrangement would you have (where would you have people sit—at a high table, for example)?
6. What would you give people to eat with?

Tell each other about the meals that you have planned. Then ask your partner whether the dinner that you have planned is like one that would be served in his or her country.

CHAPTER

5 Sports

VOCABULARY

Study the following vocabulary.

Nouns

champion – person who is better than others at a sport

coach – person who helps the players on a team learn to play better and who tells them what to do during a game

contest – game that people are trying to win

foul – something that a player does that is against the rules

goal – "object" of a sport or other effort (for example, the goal of basketball is to throw the ball through the basket)

official – person who decides whether the players are obeying the rules

opponent – a person or team who is playing or fighting against another

penalty – punishment that someone is given for not following the rules or for doing something wrong

spectator – person who watches a sport

stadium – a large field with high rows of seats around it, in which games such as football and soccer are played

trophy – prize for winning a sport (for example, a metal statue)

uniform – certain kind of clothes that the players of a team wear

victory – winning a contest

Verbs

to beat – to do better than (someone) in a game or sport

to cheer – to clap or yell for a player or team

to tie – to make the same score as the player or team that one is playing against

to train – to teach someone a skill, such as how to play a sport or game

Adjectives

competitive – eager to win; trying very hard to win

defensive – in a position to keep another person or team from making points

offensive – in a position to make points

The Soccer Game

With your partner, take turns reading lines of the following dialogue. Choose the correct vocabulary word to put into each blank.

    (*Ellen and Diana arrive at the soccer game. It has already begun. They look around for seats.*)

ELLEN: So this is your first time at a soccer game. I think you'll really enjoy it. Let's sit here with the Australians. I like their team. They always

play hard. They're very _____.

DIANA: What about their _____? Who are they?

ELLEN: They're from Britain. They're a good team, too. By the way, do you

understand the _____ of the game?

DIANA: Yes, it's simply to get the ball into the net, isn't it? And it looks like somebody's doing that right now. Oh, yea, yea! Oh, oh. Why are the

other _____ looking at me like that?

ELLEN: It's my fault. I should have told you that the Australian players are the ones wearing the green and gold uniforms. You were

_____ for the British team.

opponents – persons or teams that are playing or fighting against another person or team

cheering – clapping or yelling for a player or team

competitive – eager to win; trying very hard to win

goal – "object" of a sport

spectators – persons who are watching a sport

A Champion's Memories

Cover the left-hand side of the page with a piece of paper. Then, listen as your teacher reads the dialogue. After each section is read, choose the best definition for the boldface word.

(Jane is visiting the home of her new friend, Barbara. She sees something interesting in the living room.)

1.   JANE: Oh, what a beautfiul statue!
    BARBARA: Thank you. It's a **trophy** I won years ago for running.

1. **trophy** means:
   a. small amount of money
   b. statue given as a prize
   c. Olympic gold medal

2.   JANE: You must have been a good runner.
    BARBARA: Yes, I was, if I do say so myself. I was **champion** in the half-mile at the Oregon State Track Meet for two years.

2. **champion** means:
   a. person who is best at a certain sport
   b. person who sees that the other players are obeying the rules
   c. person who is unable to play a sport or game

3.   JANE: Did you ever lose a race?
    BARBARA: I lost once or twice. But I usually **beat** my opponents.

3. **beat** means:
   a. did better than
   b. did the same as
   c. did worse than

4.   JANE: It must have felt great to win.
    BARBARA: You're right about that. **Victory** is always a good feeling.

4. **Victory** means:
   a. losing a sport or contest
   b. winning a sport or contest
   c. learning a sport

5.   JANE: Do you still run?
   BARBARA: No, I haven't since I hurt my knee five years ago, but I still keep my old **uniform** hanging in the closet. Maybe you'd like to see it.

5. **uniform** means:
   a. photographs of someone playing a sport
   b. set of clothes worn for a game or sport
   c. players whom one has played against

Some Favorite Sports in the United States

You or your partner should read the following story. Use the other words in the sentence to help you understand the boldface words.

One of the things Americans like to do best when they're relaxing is to watch sports. Two of their favorite sports are baseball and basketball.

Baseball is played mainly in the spring, and it is played outdoors in a **stadium.** It is not a violent sport. But sometimes, the players get angry, and once in a while they get in fights or even argue with the **official.** Then they are given a **penalty** and they must leave the game. Lots of people get really excited watching baseball. They don't get bored even though it is a slow-moving game.

Basketball is usually played in the winter. Unlike baseball, it is usually played indoors. In basketball, it is a **foul** for players to push or run into each other. The penalty for a foul is that a member of the other team is given the ball to throw into the basket.

Basketball is a much faster-moving game than baseball. A team can be in an **offensive** position and trying to put the ball in the basket at one moment. At the next moment, the team is in a **defensive** position and trying to keep the other team from making points. Sometimes the score in basketball can be very high. Each team can have about 100 points.

When the teams in either of these games are equal, the **contest** can be very exciting. Of course, the spectators don't want the teams to **tie.** They want their own team to win.

The best basketball and baseball players become very well-known. And the **coaches** of good teams are sometimes as popular as the players. People understand that even great players do better when they are **trained** by a good coach.

If you don't understand the meaning of the boldface words, review their definitions at the beginning of this chapter.

With your partner, use the words beneath each picture to describe it.

official
penalty
foul
defensive
offensive

stadium
coach
contest
to tie
to train

CONVERSATION
What's Wrong Here?

*With the other members of your group, name the **five** things that are wrong in each picture. Use some of the words listed here. Write down your answers.*

penalty

offensive

goal

defensive

uniform

foul

competitive

Tell the class what's wrong in one or two of the pictures.

Sports in Your Country

What are sports like in your country? With the other members of your group, take turns reading the following questions. After each question is read, every group member should answer about his or her country.

National Sport

1. What is the national sport in your country? What is its **goal?**
2. Do both men and women play the national sport?

Men's and Women's Sports

1. What sports do women like to play in your country?
2. What sports do men like to play in your country?

Customs and Traditions

1. Which traditional sports are still played in your country?
2. Are there any sports which people in your country once played, but which are now against the law for religious or moral reasons? Which ones?
3. Is it legal for people in your country to bet money on sports events? Which ones?

Winning and Rewards

1. How do people **cheer** when their player or team does well at a sports event? For example, in the United States, people clap, shout, and whistle.
2. How famous and important do sports **champions** become in your country? For example, in the United States, everyone *recognizes* some **champions** of sports like football and basketball, and they often become movie stars or have their pictures used in advertisements. What about the **coaches** who **train** great players? How famous and important do they become?
3. What kinds of **trophies** do people receive for winning at a sport in your country?
4. In which sports do players receive a lot of money for **beating** their **opponents?**

Sports Values

What are your sports values? When your teacher asks the following questions, share your opinions with the class.

National Sport

1. What are the different national sports of the students in this class? Which is the most violent?
2. Should both men and women play all these national sports?

Men's and Women's Sports

1. Should women be allowed to play any sport that they want to?
2. Should men and women be allowed to play sports together?

Customs and *Traditions*

1. Is it important for a country to continue to play traditional sports?
2. Should any sport be against the law? Why or why not?

Winning and Reward

1. Is it right for people to make large amounts of money because they are very good at a sport? Why or why not?

Name the Sport

Student with a Sport: When a teacher asks you to get up in front of the class, secretly choose a sport, and do not tell anyone what it is yet. Answer only "yes" or "no" when the other students ask you about your sport. If they do not guess your sport within twenty questions tell them what it is.

Class: Try to guess what the sport of the student in front of the room is. Ask only questions that can be answered "yes" or "no."

For example:

1. Do you play this sport in a **stadium?**
2. Is the sport watched by many **spectators?**
3. Is it possible for teams to **tie** in this sport?
4. Do the **officials** in this sport wear black and white **uniforms?**

You may ask only twenty questions.

A Sports Event in Your Country

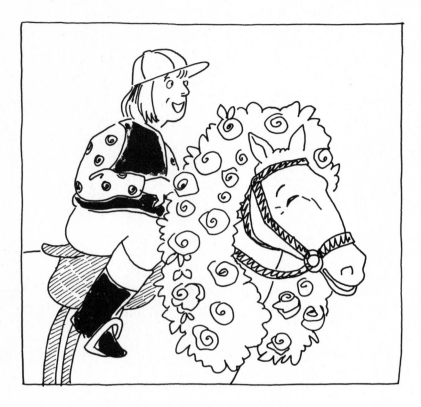

What is a famous sports event in your country? Tell your partner:

1. what it is.
2. where it is held.
3. at what time of the year it is held.
4. how often it is held.
5. whether there are any special *traditions* (such as singing special songs) before this sports event.
6. what happens during this sports event.
7. what happens after this sports event.
8. what kinds of **trophies** or other awards are given to the winners of this **contest.**
9. what the **spectators** do to *celebrate* the **victory** of their team.

Tell the class something that you learned about another country from a group member.

CHAPTER

6 Dating and Marriage

VOCABULARY

Study the following vocabulary.

Nouns

alimony – money that a husband pays his wife (or that a wife pays her husband) after they have separated

bride – woman who is about to be or has just been married

couple – man and woman who are married or who are dating

dating service – agency that helps men and women find people to date

groom – man who is about to be or has just been married

honeymoon – vacation taken by a man and woman right after they get married

marriage partner – husband or wife

marriage role – the way one acts and the responsibilities one has in a marriage

matchmaker – person who *introduces* two people to each other, hoping that they will get married

newlywed – person who has recently gotten married

reception – party held after a wedding

wedding – celebration in which two people get married

wedding anniversary – day which is exactly a year or exactly a certain number
of years after someone has gotten married

Verbs

to elope – to run away secretly in order to get married

to propose – to ask someone to get married

to separate – to stop living together

Adjectives

compatible – well-matched; able to live together happily

engaged – having agreed to marry a certain person

Expressions

to fall in love – to begin to be in love

to get along – to maintain a friendly relationship

A Nice Couple

With your partner, take turns reading lines of the following dialogue. Choose the correct vocabulary word to put into each blank.

(*Allen and his wife, Mary Ann, are lying on the beach. They are talking.*)

ALLEN: How are the Browns doing? I heard that they were having some
problems.

MARY ANN: That's true. They were having some disagreements over their

_____. She's a doctor and makes a lot of money, and he's been unemployed for several months. He hasn't liked staying home and doing the housework.

ALLEN: Are they _____ any better?

MARY ANN: No, they've _____ for a few weeks, and they're thinking about getting a divorce.

ALLEN: Well, I don't think she'll want to get one. She'd probably have

to pay him _____.

MARY ANN: You may be right. Anyway, I hope they'll stay together. They're

a nice _____.

separated – stopped living together

getting along – maintaining a friendly relationship

marriage roles – the way people act and the responsibilities they have in a marriage

couple – man and woman who are married or who are dating

alimony – money that a husband pays a wife, or that a wife pays a husband, after they have separated

A Lovely Bride

Cover the left-hand side of the page with a piece of paper. Then, listen as your teacher reads the dialogue. After each section is read, choose the best definition for the boldface word.

(Jan and Audrey, who are roommates, are sitting in a church. They are waiting for their friend Margo to be married.)

1.   JAN: The music's starting to play!
    AUDREY: Yeah, the **wedding's** about to begin. It's hard to believe that Margo's getting married.

                (a few minutes later)

1. **wedding** means:
   a. party held before a marriage ceremony
   b. marriage ceremony
   c. trip taken after a marriage ceremony

2.   JAN: Doesn't Margo look beautiful?
    AUDREY: Yes, she is a lovely **bride.**

2. **bride** means:
   a. little girl who carries flowers in a marriage ceremony
   b. mother of the woman who is getting married
   c. woman who is getting married

3.   JAN: Have you met the guy she's marrying?
    AUDREY: No, I don't know the **groom.** But he looks like a nice person.

3. **groom** means:
   a. father of the woman who is getting married
   b. best friend of the man who is getting married
   c. man who is getting married

4. JAN: Well, we'll get a chance to meet him in an hour or so.

AUDREY: You must be kidding. We won't have a chance to *get acquainted* with him at the **reception.** He'll be too busy cutting the wedding cake and having his picture taken with Margo.

4. **reception** means:
   a. party held right after a marriage ceremony
   b. party held before a marriage ceremony
   c. party held several weeks after a marriage ceremony

5. JAN: Yeah. You're right about that.

AUDREY: I know what we could do, though. Why don't we take them out for dinner next week when they get back from their **honeymoon?**

5. **honeymoon** means:
   a. trip taken by a man and woman right after they get married
   b. trip taken by a man and woman before they get married
   c. trip taken by a man and woman a long time after they get married

Marriage in the United States

You or your partner should read the following story. Use the other words in the sentence to help you understand the boldface words.

Many single people in the United States have trouble finding a **marriage partner.** In the past, sometimes friends would help by becoming **matchmakers.** They would *introduce* a man and woman, and sometimes the man and woman would **fall in love** and get married.

But today, many people pay companies called **dating services** to help them find partners. And even if the dating service does not always find them someone to marry, it at least finds them someone to date.

Getting married has changed in some ways. In the past, the man **proposed** to the woman. But now sometimes the woman asks the man to marry her. After the couple decides to marry, the man gives the woman a ring. She wears it on her left hand to show that they **are engaged.** Sometimes the man and woman **elope.** When they run away and get married privately, their parents are often disappointed because they wanted their children to have a big wedding.

When they are married, both **newlyweds** often work because they need two paychecks to pay their bills. But sometimes they still have money problems. And sometimes the partners find that they just aren't **compatible.** So, for many people, marriage ends in divorce. Yet, some people stay together long enough to *celebrate* their fiftieth or seventy-fifth **wedding anniversary.**

If you don't understand the meaning of the boldface words, review their definitions at the beginning of this chapter.

With your partner use the words beneath each picture to describe it.

dating service

marriage partner

newlyweds

compatible

to fall in love

wedding anniversary

to propose

engaged

matchmaker

to elope

CONVERSATION
What Should These Couples Do?

With the other members of your group, read each problem. Put yourself into the situation, and imagine how you would feel if you were each of the people involved in the problem. With the other group members, try to think of as many solutions as possible.

Then, discuss the advantages and disadvantages of each solution. Decide for yourself which one you prefer. Explain to the other students why you think as you do. As a group, try to come to an agreement as to which solution is best.

Situation 1

Dan **has fallen in love** with Barbara. They both want to get married, but Dan doesn't want a big **wedding.** He wants to **elope.** His family lives in a faraway city. They can't afford to pay for any part of the **wedding** or even to come to it.

If Dan and Barbara have a big **wedding,** they will have to wait six or eight weeks before they can get married. Barbara wants special wedding rings for them both, and it will take several weeks to have them made. Dan wants to get married right away so that he and Barbara can move to another city, where he has been offered a good job at a bank.

Barbara has always wanted a big **wedding** with a fine **reception.** Her parents have a lot of money (her father is the president of the largest bank in the city), and they would be able to pay for these things easily. But Barbara feels sympathy for Dan and understands how he feels.

Situation 2

Donna is worried that Jerry will forget their **wedding anniversary** again this year. She'll feel terrible if he does, but she doesn't want to tell him when it is. Also, she'd like a different kind of gift this year—not a piece of kitchen equipment again. She'd like Jerry to take her on a trip.

Jerry knows that his **wedding anniversary** will be soon, but he can't *recall* the exact date. He doesn't want to ask Donna, because she'd feel bad that he'd forgotten again.

He's having trouble deciding what kind of gift to get her. He usually gives her kitchen equipment, but he's not sure that she really likes practical gifts. He doesn't want to ask her what she'd like, because then she'd think that he had no imagination.

Situation 3

Richard wants to marry Karen, but he doesn't know whether he should. Karen wants to keep working after they get married, but he doesn't want her to. He is a doctor and he makes a lot of money, so he doesn't think that Karen needs to work. Also, he has two children (a three-year-old and a four-year-old) from an earlier marriage. Right now, they are in a nursery school, but Richard thinks that if he and Karen got married, she should stay home with them. Richard has one more fear: he is afraid that if he and Karen get a divorce, he will have to pay a lot of **alimony.** He has worked hard for his money, and he doesn't want to lose it.

Karen has a good job in advertising and doesn't want to leave it. If she quits, she might never be able to find such a good job again. Besides, she thinks that Richard is working too many hours. If she keeps working after the **wedding,** maybe he will be able to work less. Karen understands Richard's fears, but she thinks that he has no need to worry. She feels that they **get along** so well that they'll never get a divorce.

Describe the problems and solutions to the class.

A Dating Service

You and your group work for LaMont's **Dating Service.** *People come to your service because they want to find someone to date. But before you can introduce one of your customers to another customer, you must ask him or her some questions to find out what kind of person he or she would like to date. With your coworkers, write a set of questions, or questionnaire, for your customers to answer. Make up new questions like the first question in each category. Write your group's questions in your book.*

When your group has finished making up its questionnaire, leave your group and sit with one person from another group. This person has come to your **dating service** *to find someone to date. Find out what kind of person your customer would like to date by asking him or her the questions on your questionnaire. Write down his or her answers.*

Reverse roles.

Dating Questionnaire

Beliefs

1. How important is it for the person whom you date to be religious?

   _____

2. _____

_____

3. _____

_____

Habits

1. How would you feel about dating a person who smokes? _____

_____

2. _____

_____

3. _____

_____

Personality

1. How would you feel about dating a person who talks all the time?

_____

2. _____

_____

3. _____

_____

Interests

1. What kinds of things do you like to do in your free time? _____

_____

2. _____

_____

3. _____

_____

Tell the class a few things that you have learned about your partner.

Getting Ready for Marriage

Many people think that a man and a woman should have achieved certain things and should agree on certain subjects before they get married. Think of possible answers to each part of the following three questions. Discuss your answers with the other members of your group. Agree upon one answer for each part, and write it in your book.

1. *What should a man have achieved before he gets married?*

   material possessions (for example, maybe a man should own a house before he marries) _____

   _____

   educational *background* (for example, maybe a man should have a college educa-

   tion before he marries) _____

   _____

   travel _____

   _____

   employment _____

   _____

   skills _____

   _____

   other _____

   _____

2. *What should a woman have achieved before she gets married?*

   material possessions _____

   _____

   educational *background* _____

   _____

   travel _____

   _____

employment _____

_____

skills _____

_____

other _____

_____

3. *What kinds of things should a* **couple** *agree on before marriage?*

money _____

_____

children _____

_____

work _____

_____

cooking and cleaning in the home _____

_____

social activities _____

_____

other _____

_____

Tell the class your answers for some of the categories.

Marriage around the World

Follow along as the teacher reads the examples and the questions formed from them. Ask the teacher for more examples if you do not understand how to form the questions.

Example 1: Find the country where people **are engaged** for the longest time.
Question: How long **are** people **engaged** in your country?

Example 2: Find the country where education is the most important quality in choosing a **marriage partner**.

Question: How important is education in choosing a **marriage partner** in your country?

*When your teacher assigns you **one** of the following directions, make it into a question. Then, walk around the room and ask the other students your question. When you think that you have found the country that your direction asks for, write it on the line beneath the direction.*

1. Find the country where women get married the youngest. Find the country where women get married the oldest.

   _____

   _____

2. Find the country where men get married the youngest. Find the country where men get married the oldest.

   _____

   _____

3. Find the country where it is most common for parents to act as **matchmakers** to find their son or daughter a **marriage partner.** Find the country where it is the least common.

   _____

   _____

4. Find the country where there is the most divorce. Find the country where there is the least divorce.

   _____

   _____

5. Find the country where it is most important to parents for their children to marry people of the same *nationality*.

   _____

   _____

6. Find the country where people **are separated** for the longest time before they get a divorce. Find the country where they **are separated** the shortest time.

   _____

   _____

7. Find the country where it is easiest for two people to get a divorce when they are not **compatible.** Find the country where it is the most difficult.

_____

_____

8. Find the country where **couples** are most free to choose their own **marriage roles.** Find the country where they are the least free.

_____

_____

9. Find the country where it is most acceptable for a woman to **propose** to a man.

_____

_____

10. Find the country where some family members are most strongly forbidden to marry before other family members do.

_____

_____

Tell the class what country (or countries) you have found and why you chose it (them) as your answer.

Wedding Traditions

*With the other members of your group, look at the following pictures. They show things that are done before and after a **wedding** in the United States. Take turns reading the questions beneath each picture.*

After each question is read, answer it together. Use the following words in describing the pictures:

> **to fall in love**
> **engaged**
> **bride**
> **groom**
> **wedding**
> **newlywed**
> **reception**
> **honeymoon**

Before the Wedding

1. Describe what is happening in the picture.
2. What is a *similar tradition* in your own country?
3. How is it like the *tradition* in the picture? How is it different?

1. Describe what is happening in the picture.
2. What is a *similar tradition* in your own country?
3. How is it like the *tradition* in the picture? How is it different?

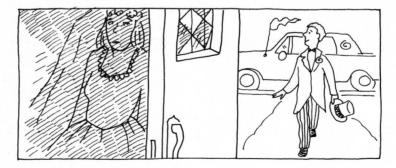

1. Describe what is happening in the picture.
2. What is a *similar tradition* in your own country?
3. How is it like the *tradition* in the picture? How is it different?

1. Describe what is happening in the picture.
2. What is a *similar tradition* in your own country?
3. How is it like the *tradition* in the picture? How is it different?

After the Wedding

1. Describe what is happening in the picture.
2. What is a *similar tradition* in your own country?
3. How is it like the *tradition* in the picture? How is it different?

1. Describe what is happening in the picture.
2. What is a *similar tradition* in your own country?
3. How is it like the *tradition* in the picture? How is it different?

Tell the class what wedding traditions *are popular in your country.*

CHAPTER
7 Family

VOCABULARY

Study the following vocabulary.

Nouns

ancestor – a family member such as a great-great-grandmother or great-great-grand-father (but not a great-great-uncle or great-great-aunt) who lived a long time ago

extended family – a mother and father and their children, but also aunts, uncles, and grandparents

family history – the history of the family; the things that have happened to oneself and one's ancestors

generation – age group that people belong to (for example, parents belong to one generation and their children belong to another)

heirloom – something, such as a ring or piece of furniture, that once belonged to one's ancestor

nuclear family – a mother and father and their children, but not aunts, uncles, cousins, or grandparents

nursing home – special home or hospital where older people are taken care of

relative – family member (for example, a brother, grandmother, or aunt)

single-parent family – family in which only one parent lives with the children

Verbs

to inherit – to receive (a gift) from a relative, especially one who has died

to mind – to obey (one's parents or grandparents)

to neglect – to ignore; not to pay attention to

to spoil – to cause (a child) not to care about the needs of others and not to accept responsibility

to support – to pay for (someone's) expenses

Adjectives

elderly – aged; old

permissive – allowing (someone) a lot of freedom

strict – strong or firm in making someone obey rules

Expressions

to grow up – to go from being a small child to being an adult

to hand (something) **down** – to give (something of one's own) to a younger relative, especially after one's death

to take care of – to provide food and other necessary things for

Grandmother's Ring

With your partner, take turns reading lines of the following dialogue. Choose the correct vocabulary word to put into each blank.

(*Victoria, a young university student, is visiting with her grandmother. She notices a beautiful gold ring on the older woman's hand.*)

VICTORIA: Oh, grandmother! What a beautiful ring you're wearing. Is it old?

GRANDMOTHER: Yes, Victoria. It's an _____ . It's been in our family for over 100 years.

VICTORIA: Really? Which one of our _____ did it first belong to?

GRANDMOTHER: It belonged to my grandmother. It was her wedding ring. My grandfather was a sea captain, and he met my grandmother when his ship sailed to the island where she lived.

                 My mother _____ the ring from my grandmother, and later she gave it to me.

VICTORIA: How interesting! Wearing the ring must make you think about

                 our _____ a lot.

GRANDMOTHER: It does. And I wanted you to know this story because one

                 day I'm going to _____ the ring to you.

family history – history of a family

heirloom – something that once belonged to a relative who lived in the past

hand down – give (something belonging to oneself) to a younger relative

inherited – received (a gift) from a relative

ancestors – relatives who lived a long time ago

A Hardworking Mother

Cover the left-hand side of the page with a piece of paper. Then, listen as your teacher reads the dialogue. After each section is read, choose the best definition for the boldface word.

(Jim and Karen are relaxing in Jim's living room. They have been telling each other about their lives.)

1. KAREN: Did you live with both your parents when you were little?

   JIM: No, my father died when I was very young, so I grew up in a **single-parent family.**

   1. **single-parent family** means:
      a. family that has only one parent living in the home
      b. family that has both parents living in the home
      c. family that has one child living in the home

2. KAREN: Did your mother work?

   JIM: Yes, she worked in an office to **support** my brother and me.

   2. **support** means:
      a. stay with
      b. pay for the expenses of
      c. spend time with

3. KAREN: It must have been difficult for her.

   JIM: It was. After a long day at her job, she came home and cooked our dinner and helped us with our homework. And **taking care of** us wasn't easy.

3. **taking care of** means:
   a. providing food and care for
   b. playing with
   c. relaxing with

4. KAREN: Didn't your mother have anyone to help her with the cooking and cleaning?

   JIM: No, she did it all by herself. She must have been tired a lot, but she never **neglected** us. In fact, she spent almost all her free time with us.

4. **neglected** means:
   a. fed
   b. ignored
   c. talked to

5. KAREN: You didn't have any grandparents or aunts or uncles who could have helped?

   JIM: We had **relatives,** but they lived in other states, so our mother had to do everything alone.

5. **relatives** means:
   a. neighbors
   b. close or distant family members
   c. close friends

Changes in the American Family

You or your partner should read the following story. Use the other words in the sentence to help you understand the boldface words.

In the nineteenth century in the United States, it was not unusual for **extended families** of uncles, aunts, cousins, and grandparents to live together in the same home. Then, in this century, **nuclear families** became popular. Only the parents and their children lived together.

Recently, in the United States, many parents and children have begun living with grandparents again. Often, parents and children don't want to send their parents and grandparents to a special **nursing home** for older people. They think it is better to take care of the **elderly** person at home.

Of course, there can be problems when people of three **generations** live in the same home. Grandparents are often more **permissive** than parents, and they let children do what they want. But most American parents feel that it is better to be **strict;** they feel that children should follow rules. Parents think that grandparents who don't make children **mind** will **spoil** them. Then the children won't obey anyone as they are **growing up.**

But having grandparents in the home can also be fun. For example, everyone enjoys the stories that older people tell and the interesting things that they can teach the other family members. Americans are learning that having elderly people in the home can be a wonderful experience.

If you don't understand the meaning of the boldface words, review their definitions at the beginning of this chapter.

With your partner, use the words beneath each picture to describe it.

permissive
strict
to mind
to spoil
to grow up

nuclear family
extended family
nursing home
elderly
generation

CONVERSATION
Who's Responsible?

With the other members of your group, look at the following pictures. Then, take turns reading the questions beneath them. After each question is read, answer it together. Use the following words in describing the pictures:

elderly

single-parent family

to support

to take care of

to neglect

1. What is happening in the picture?
2. What responsibility is suggested by the picture?
3. Who do you think should have the responsibility, and why?
4. How do you think most people in your country would feel about this situation? Who would they think should have the responsibility?

1. What is happening in the picture?
2. What responsibility is suggested by the picture?
3. Who do you think should have the responsibility, and why?
4. How do you think most people in your country would feel about this situation? Who would they think should have the responsibility?

1. What is happening in the picture?
2. What responsibility is suggested by the picture?
3. Who do you think should have the responsibility, and why?
4. How do you think most people in your country would feel about this situation? Who would they think should have the responsibility?

1. What is happening in the picture?
2. What responsibility is suggested by the picture?
3. Who do you think should have the responsibility, and why?
4. How do you think most people in your country would feel about this situation? Who would they think should have the responsibility?

1. What is happening in the picture?
2. What responsibility is suggested by the picture?
3. Who do you think should have the responsibility, and why?
4. How do you think most people in your country would feel about this situation? Who would they think should have the responsibility?

An Interesting Ancestor

*Do you have an interesting **family history**? Try to recall a story about one of your **ancestors**. (If you do not know much about your **ancestors**, you should talk about a living family member.) Prepare your story at home, and try to find a picture of the person to show the other students. Then, tell your story to the class.*

Taking Care of a Young Relative

Your brother and his wife are going on a world cruise, and they have asked you and your partner to **take care of** *their sixteen-year-old daughter while they are gone. Together, agree upon rules that you will have your niece obey. (In some cases, you may want to be* **strict,** *and in other cases, you may want to be* **permissive** *and let the girl make her own decisions.)*

1. Home responsibilities
2. Personal habits
   a. studying
   b. smoking
   c. drinking
   d. dress
   e. movies that she is allowed to see, and books and magazines that she is allowed to read
3. Social activities
   a. dating
   b. friends that she is allowed to spend time with

Tell the class some of the rules that you have made.

An Heirloom

What is an **heirloom** *that has been* **handed down** *to someone in your family? (If nothing has been* **handed down** *yet, you may tell about something that will be* **handed down** *in the future.) Tell your partner:*

1. what the **heirloom** is
2. where it came from (for example, if it belonged to your grandfather, where did he get it?)
3. which older family member gave (or will give) the **heirloom** to a younger member of your family
4. who **inherited** (or will **inherit**) the **heirloom**
5. why the **heirloom** is special

Disagreeing with Family Members

With your partner(s), act out a role play.

Situation 1

Daughter-in-law: You're a doctor. Your job is very important to you, and your husband thinks that it is fine for you to work. But your in-laws want you to stop working because you're gone from home too much. Your job is too important for you to give up. And you feel that your children are being well **taken care of** by the babysitter.

Son: You feel that you need the money your wife makes to help **support** the family. You don't care if the house isn't very neat. And you think that the babysitter does a good job of **taking care of** the children. You're proud of your wife's occupation and of her.

Mother: You think that your daughter-in-law should spend more time with her husband and children. You think that the babysitter is **spoiling** the children. Now, they won't **mind** their parents.

Father: You think that a wife's most important responsibility is to **take care of** her husband and children. You feel that your daughter-in-law shouldn't work until the children have **grown up.** Also, you don't think she's being a good homemaker.

Situation 2

Son: You want to become an artist, but your parents would like you to become a doctor. You don't want to become a doctor because you don't care about money and you don't want to **take care of** people. The only thing that you would like to do is paint. You love making beautiful pictures and living a free kind of life. You wouldn't like having the long hours and the responsibilities of working in a hospital.

Father: You want your son to become a doctor. He will make a lot of money and people will *respect* him if he becomes a doctor. You tell him that you will pay for him to go to medical school, but not to art school.

Mother: You think your son should do what his father tells him. You think that your son is too young to know what's best for him. You will be very proud of him if he becomes a doctor.

Situation 3

Donna: You want to get married, but your parents are unhappy with the man you have chosen because he is very poor. You don't care about having a lot of money. You're sure that you'll be happy in any home with your future husband. You have *fallen in love* with this man and want to spend the rest of your life with him.

Mother: You don't think that it would be a good idea for your daughter to marry the man who has asked her, because he is very poor and has an unimportant job. Your daughter's future husband doesn't have enough education to get the kind of job you'd like for him to get. You are afraid your daughter will *elope* with this man.

Father: You think that the man whom your daughter wants to marry probably won't be able to buy her a nice home. Maybe she will have to live in a bad part of town. You're sure that if she waits, another man will soon come along. You think that she shouldn't marry this man.

Situation 4

Grandmother: You live with your children and grandchildren, but some of them want to put you in a **nursing home.** You are sorry that you have been so much trouble to the family, but you want to stay with them. You think that maybe they could hire a nurse to **take care of** you. You are afraid that if you go to a **nursing home** the family will seldom come to visit you.

Mr. Andrews: Your wife has a lot of work to do and cannot **take care of** your mother very well. You would like to get a nurse to **take care of** her in your home, but it would cost too much money. You think that if your mother goes to a home for old people, it will seem strange to her at first, but she will get *used to* it later.

Mrs. Andrews: You love your husband's mother, but it has become very difficult for you to **take care of** her. You wonder whether she would like to go to a **nursing home.** You feel that she might like the home, because she could *get acquainted* with new friends of her own **generation.**

Terry: You feel sad that your grandmother might be put into a **nursing home.** You want her to stay with the family. You've enjoyed living in an **extended family** more than in a **nuclear family.** You've decided that you will help **take care of** your grandmother so that she can stay with you. You wonder how your parents would like to be put into a home for old people.

CHAPTER
8 Travel

VOCABULARY

Study the following vocabulary.

Nouns

accommodation – lodging, place to stay (such as a hotel room)

contraband – goods that one tries to bring secretly into a country without paying duty

customs – the place where government workers look through people's luggage to see that they are not bringing taxable things into a country

destination – place that one is traveling to

duty – tax that must be paid on things that are brought into or taken out of a country

fare – price that one pays to ride in an airplane, on a ship, or on another means of transportation

foreign exchange – office where one goes to change one's money for the money of another country

itinerary – schedule listing the times and dates when one will visit different places during a trip

reservation – agreement that a hotel room, plane ticket, or something else will be saved for a person until he or she asks for it

sight-seeing – visiting interesting places in order to see interesting things

souvenir – something that one buys (often during a trip) to help one remember the place visited

travel arrangements – travel plans and preparations

vagabond – person who travels from place to place without a particular purpose

Verbs

to board – to get onto (a ship, airplane, bus, or train)

to smuggle – to bring (something) into a country illegally

Adjectives

cosmopolitan – sophisticated; knowing a lot about the world

round-trip – to a place and back again; two-way

weary – very, very tired

Expressions

jet lag – the tired feeling that one has after traveling by plane for many hours

to travel light – to travel with only a small amount of luggage

A Trip to Europe

With your partner, take turns reading lines of the following dialogue. Choose the correct vocabulary word to put into each blank.

(*Jackie and Rosemary are high school teachers. They are eating lunch in the school cafeteria.*)

ROSEMARY: Hey, Jackie. How'd you like to go to Europe this summer? We

could just be _____ _____ and go wherever we wanted whenever we wanted.

JACKIE: Well, I don't know about that. I'd prefer it if we had some

_____. I'd like to go to France first, and then Spain and England. What do you think about that idea?

ROSEMARY: I guess that would be OK. But I think we should begin planning right away. We need to get travelers' checks before going. Then we can just change our money in each country at the

_____.

JACKIE: That sounds good to me. There's no one I'd rather go with than you to see some *exotic* places. You speak so many languages, and

you're really _____.

ROSEMARY: I'm so glad you're going to go with me, too. You're so responsible. The last time I went to Europe with someone, she tried to

_____ perfume into the United States, and we got into trouble with customs!

itinerary – schedule of a trip

smuggle – bring (something) into a country illegally

foreign exchange – office where one goes to *exchange* one's money for the money of another country

vagabonds – people who travel from place to place without a particular purpose

cosmopolitan – sophisticated; knowing a lot about the world

A Helpful Desk Clerk

Cover the left-hand side of the page with a piece of paper. Then, listen as your teacher reads the dialogue. After each section is read, choose the best definition for the boldface word.

(*Ben, a lawyer, has just arrived in a foreign country. He comes into a hotel carrying several heavy suitcases.*)

1.   BEN: Could I have a room, please?
DESK CLERK: I'm sorry. We don't have any **accommodations.**

1. **accommodations** means:
   a. ideas about the places to visit in a city
   b. places to stay
   c. rooms for several people

2.   BEN: You're kidding! I just got off the plane, and I'm really tired.
DESK CLERK: That's too bad! I know what it's like to have **jet lag!**

2. **jet lag** means:
   a. a long trip by train
   b. a tired feeling from traveling by plane
   c. a relaxed feeling that one has while one is on vacation

3.   **BEN:** I can't believe that all your rooms are *occupied*. Is there some especially interesting event happening here right now?

     DESK CLERK: Well, yes. Don't you know about the wine *festival*? And, of course, the countryside is really pretty in the fall, so a lot of tourists come for **sight-seeing.**

3. **sight-seeing** means:
  a. seeing movies and plays
  b. looking at maps and travel books
  c. visiting places to see interesting things

4.   **BEN:** Oh, I didn't know about that. My travel agent told me I'd have no problem finding a place to stay this month.

     DESK CLERK: Maybe next time you should have someone else make your **travel arrangements.**

4. **travel arrangements** means:
  a. hotels where one stays
  b. plans as to where to stay and how to travel
  c. money used for travel

5.   **BEN:** You're probably right. Well, I guess I'll just have to go to another hotel! But I sure don't like the idea of having to carry all these suitcases.

     DESK CLERK: Well, if I may make a suggestion, I think that next time you should **travel light.**

5. **travel light** means:
  a. travel by plane
  b. travel with a small amount of baggage
  c. travel a short distance

A Misunderstanding at Customs

You or your partner should read the following story. Use the other words in the sentence to help you understand the boldface words.

When you travel, you can have the most unusual problems. Like the one I had after my trip to Switzerland last year. I went there to ski, and that was how I spent almost all my time. I did buy some **souvenirs** for my friends, but I couldn't buy anything expensive, because it cost so much to ski and to pay the **round-trip fare.**

My **reservation** was for only three weeks, and before I knew it, it was time to come home. After I **boarded** the plane I was so excited about telling my friends about my trip that I couldn't sleep at all until I reached New York, my **destination.**

When I was coming back through **customs** in New York, I was wearing a Swiss watch that I'd bought in the United States. But the customs agent thought it was **contraband** that I was bringing back from Switzerland. After the long flight, I was too **weary** to argue with him, so I ended up paying **duty** on a watch I already owned!

If you don't understand the meaning of the boldface words, review their definitions at the beginning of this chapter.

With your partner, use the words beneath each picture to describe it.

to board
reservation
destination
round-trip
fare

customs
souvenir
contraband
weary
duty

CONVERSATION
An Interesting City to Visit

What city in your country would people like to visit? Tell your partner:

1. its name
2. its geography (oceans, lakes, mountains, rivers)
3. things to see there
4. sports that are done there
5. its cultural attractions (music, art, etc.)
6. other interesting things about it

Finding a Traveling Companion

You and your group work for Magic Carpet Travel Agency. Some of the people who come to your agency want you to help them find other people to travel with. But before you can do that, you must ask them some questions to find out what kind of people they would like to travel with. With your coworkers, write a set of questions, or questionnaire, for your customers to answer. Make up two new questions for each category (the subject for the second question is already given). Write down your group's questions in your book.

When your group has finished making up its questionnaire, leave your group and sit with one person from another group. This person has come to your travel agency to find a traveling companion. Find out what kind of person your customer would like to travel with by asking him or her the questions on your questionnaire. Write down his or her answers.

Reverse roles.

Physical Description

1. *(nationality)* What *nationality* would you like your traveling companion to be?

   _____

2. (sex) _____

   _____

3. (   ) _____

   ____ ____ _____

Personality Traits

1. (independence) How would you feel about traveling with someone who needed

   you to *entertain* him or her constantly? _____

_____

2. (sense of humor) _____

_____

3. (   ) _____

_____

Personal Habits

1. Do you want to travel with someone who likes to go to bed early or someone

   who likes to stay up late? _____

   _____

2. (smoking) _____

   _____

3. (   ) _____

   _____

Activities

1. Do you like to do activities with other people or by yourself? _____

   _____

2. (active or passive activities) _____

   _____

3. _____

   _____

Travel Arrangements

1. What countries would you include in your **itinerary?** _____

   _____

2. **(accommodations)** _____

   _____

3. (   ) _____

_____

Tell the class a few things that you have learned about your partner.

Planning a Vacation

Part 1. *What kind of vacation would you plan for your partner? Ask him or her the following questions. Write down his or her answers.*

1. What kind of a climate do you like when you go on vacation? _____

    _____

2. What kind of surroundings (mountains, trees, beaches, lakes) do you like?

    _____

3. Do you like to go to a place that has a lot of people in it or just a few

    people? _____

    _____

4. Do you like to do a lot of activities or relax and do few activities?_____

    _____

5. What kinds of sports do you like to play on vacation? _____

    _____

6. What kinds of things do you like to see when you go to a country? _____

    _____

7. What kinds of things do you like to buy (English china, Oriental rugs, clocks,

    cars, clothes, inexpensive **souvenirs**)? _____

    _____

8. What kinds of hotels do you like to stay in? _____

    _____

9. What kinds of restaurants do you like to go to? _____

10. How interested are you in getting to know the culture (the thoughts, beliefs, and art) of a foreign country? _____ _____

Reverse roles.

Part 2. *Plan a vacation for each other. Use the information from Part 1 to help you answer the following questions.*

1. What country should you send the person to? _____ _____

2. Where in the country should you send him or her to (a big city, a medium-sized city, a small town)? _____ _____

3. What kinds of things should you plan for this person to do on his or her vacation (play a certain sport, go **sight-seeing,** buy certain things)? _____ _____

4. Where should you have the person stay (in a hotel, with a family, in a camp-ground)? _____ _____

5. Where should you have this person eat (in a fine restaurant, at a sidewalk café, in someone's home, in an informal restaurant that serves food from your partner's country)? _____ _____

6. What things can you do to help this person *get acquainted* with the people of the country and their language if he or she wants to do so? _____ _____

Tell each other about the vacations that you have planned.

Then each of you should ask the other whether he or she would enjoy this vacation.

A Useful Phrase Book

You and the other members of your group are going to write a book of useful phrases for travelers who don't speak English. Following are some situations that travelers commonly **experience***. With the other members of your group, take turns reading the situations and the examples of useful phrases beneath them. After each situation and its examples are read, make up other phrases that people in that situation might need to use. (Some of the phrases can be funny!) Write down the group's answers.*

Situation 1

Two *newlyweds* are going to New York for their *honeymoon*. They will be staying in an inexpensive hotel so that they can save money to go see some good plays.

Write some phrases that these people might need while they are staying at the hotel.

Examples:

"We wanted a room with a bath!"

"Eight suitcases! I thought we'd agreed to **travel light!**"

Situation 2

A tourist is walking around Seattle. It starts to rain. The tourist has forgotten his umbrella. He discovers that he is lost.

Write some phrases that the tourist might need from the time he discovers he is lost until the time he arrives back at his hotel.

Examples:

"Excuse me. How do I get to the Olympic Hotel?"

"Do you mind if I stand under your umbrella?"

Situation 3

A group of people who have been visiting Europe are taking a tour of London. Their bus lets them off at a restaurant for lunch. Some of the food is not very *appetizing*, the service is poor, and there are other problems.

Write some phrases that these people might need from the time they enter the restaurant until the time they leave.

Examples:

"Where's the waiter? I'm *starved*!"

"This food *tastes* a lot different from the *cuisine* we had in Paris."

Situation 4

A businesswoman is flying to Los Angeles to attend a meeting in a hotel far from the Los Angeles airport. When her plane lands, she can't find her baggage at first. In her baggage are some important papers that she will need for the meeting.

Write some phrases that the woman might need from the time she gets on her plane until the time she arrives at her meeting.

Examples:

"Excuse me. I think you've got my suitcase."

"Can you tell me where to catch a taxi?"

Situation 5

Two friends decide to be **vagabonds** for the summer. Right now, they are traveling across the United States by bus. This particular trip takes four days. It is the middle of July and the bus is very crowded with people of all ages and their baggage.

Write some phrases that the two friends might need during the bus trip.

Examples:

"Will we **ever** reach our **destination?**"

"I wish we hadn't bought a **round-trip** bus ticket. We should have spent the money for plane **fare!**"

Tell the class the phrases you have written for each situation.

Some Travel Problems

With your partner(s), act out a role play.

Situation 1

Dan: You have just arrived in a city. You have **jet lag** and you want to rest, so you go to check into a hotel. The travel agent who made your **travel arrangements** made a **reservation** for you here. But the clerk tells you that you have no **reservation.** You are upset because you are **weary,** and you think this hotel has many empty rooms.

Desk Clerk: You don't think that Dan has a **reservation.** You can't find one in the files. You think that the paper he has is for another hotel. You want him to leave because he seems to be a troublemaker.

Hotel Manager: You don't want to give Dan a room because, although you have many empty rooms now, the hotel will soon be full. There is going to be a conference of window washers. You don't want Dan to know that you have some empty rooms.

Situation 2

Susan: You are **boarding** a plane, and you go to find your seat. Your boarding pass says seat 9-E, but when you go to that seat, it is already *occupied*. You really wanted the window seat. You are angry with the airline for making a mistake. You are especially angry because this has happened to you before.

Dave: When Susan tells you that you are sitting in her seat, you realize that a mistake has been made. One of you should be sitting in 9-D. You tell Susan that you're sorry but you are not moving because it is the airline's mistake, not yours. When the flight attendant suggests that you take turns sitting by the window, you refuse.

Flight Attendant: You hear the discussion between Susan and Dave. You realize that the airline has made a mistake. You try to calm the two people down because you are afraid that they may upset the other passengers. You suggest that they take turns sitting by the window.

Situation 3

Ellen: You go to the airport to pick up a Brazilian friend, but you cannot find her. You are getting worried. Although she is very **cosmopolitan,** she cannot speak English, and has never been to this city before. You go to the baggage area to look for her. After looking for her for twenty minutes, you ask the baggage attendant whether he has seen her. You don't know why she is so hard to find, because she said she would be wearing a bright red coat and black leather jeans. You are getting worried.

Baggage attendant: You would like to help this woman, but you can't remember having seen her friend. Too many people pass through this area for you to remember them all. You suggest that Ellen look for her friend in the airport restaurant or at the **foreign exchange.**

Tourist: You hear Ellen talking to the baggage attendant. You are interested in this conversation, because you think that a Brazilian woman was on the same plane that you just got off. After listening for a couple of minutes you interrupt and ask Ellen to describe her friend. When she does, you think you may have seen her. You try to remember where.

Situation 4

Esther: You have arrived at an airport, and you are going through **customs** when a customs agent asks whether you have anything to declare. You tell him that you don't. When he finds an expensive clock in your bag, you don't want to pay **duty,** so you tell him that you brought it with you from your own country. When the customs agent doesn't believe you and wants to take the clock away, you are very upset. You looked all over Europe to find a clock like this.

Customs agent: You think that Esther is trying to **smuggle** some **contraband** into the country. You finally find a clock in her bag. You ask where it came from. You don't believe Esther when she tells you she brought the clock from her own country. You try to get her to tell you the truth. You are about to take the clock away when another traveler interrupts.

Howard: You listen to everything that happens. You think that Esther is lying, but you don't want her to lose her beautiful clock. You interrupt and give the customs agent reasons why Esther should be allowed to keep the clock.

9 Entertainment

VOCABULARY

Study the following vocabulary.

Nouns

audience – group of people who watch or listen to a performance

box office – office where tickets for a movie or play are sold

censorship – changes made in movies or TV programs so that they won't show certain things such as too much violence

channel – TV station (for example, Channel 8, 11, or 27)

commercial – TV advertisement for a product or service

critic – person who is paid to give his or her ideas about whether a movie, play, or TV show is good

curtain call – appearance by the actors on stage at the end of a play

fan – someone who is especially interested in a certain entertainer

cable TV – TV channels that one must pay to watch

performance – the singing, dancing, or acting done by an entertainer

ratings – numbers that show how many people watch each TV program

review – ideas about a movie, play, or TV show that are written or spoken by a critic

scene – one of the parts into which a movie, play, or TV show is divided; a scene contains a single action or related set of actions

sequel – movie (or book) that continues the story begun in an earlier movie (or book)

series – TV show that is shown every week

stage – raised area where actors stand when they perform in a play

TV listings – magazine or special part of a newspaper that tells what programs are being shown on TV

Verbs

to be admitted – to be let in

to applaud – to clap; to show the entertainers that they did a good job

to boo – to say "boo," an impolite way of showing the entertainers that they did a bad job

A Bad Decision

With your partner, take turns reading lines of the following dialogue. Choose the correct vocabulary word to put into each blank.

(*Carol and Ted are neighbors. They have decided to spend Saturday evening together. Right now, they are in Carol's apartment.*)

CAROL: Want to watch TV?

TED: I don't know. Do you have _____ ?

CAROL: No, I decided not to get it. It has less _____ than

regular TV, and why should I pay money just to see more violence?

TED: Well, without cable, you don't get as many

_____ . I bet you just get 6, 8, and 10, right?

CAROL: Yes, but there might be something good on, anyway. Are you sure

you don't want to look at the _____?

TED: I'm sure. Unless you have cable TV, there are too many

_____ that come on in the middle of programs.

CAROL: OK, we won't watch TV, then. But your favorite movie, *Revenge of the Potato People*, is on channel 10. Since you don't want to watch it, you can take me to the theater. I've already got the *reservations*.

TV listings – magazine or special part of the newspaper that tells what programs are being shown on TV

channels – TV stations

censorship – changes made in TV shows (or movies) so that they show less violence

cable TV – TV channels that one must pay to watch

commercials – TV advertisements

A Popular Series

Cover the left-hand side of the page with a piece of paper. Then, listen as your teacher reads the dialogue. After each section is read, choose the best definition for the boldface word.

(Two friends, Madeleine and Tim are relaxing in Madeleine's living room one evening.)

1. MADELEINE: Ooh! Quick! Turn on the TV! It's time for "Kansas City!" I missed it last week, and I was so upset.

   TIM: Were you? I've never watched this **series** before.

1. **series** means:
   a. TV show that is on every week
   b. movie that is shown on TV after it is shown in the theaters
   c. old TV show that is no longer shown on TV

2. MADELEINE: Really? I thought everybody watched it.

   TIM: Well, I've heard that it gets good **ratings,** so I guess that a lot of people do.

2. **ratings** means:
   a. TV shows that are shown on different channels, at the same time
   b. TV shows that are shown on the same evening
   c. numbers showing how many people watch a TV program

3. MADELEINE: Then why don't *you* watch it?

   TIM: Because I've read the **reviews** in the TV magazines, and they weren't good.

3. **reviews** means:
   a. plays that were written centuries ago
   b. letters written to a movie star
   c. opinions written in a magazine or newspaper about the quality of a TV show or movie

4. MADELEINE: I'm surprised to hear that.

   TIM: Well, it's true. The **critics** don't like "Kansas City" at all. They write terrible things about it.

4. **critics** means:
   a. the people who watch TV
   b. people who read a lot of movie magazines
   c. people who are paid to write or discuss their ideas about a TV show or movie

5. MADELEINE: Well, I don't pay any attention to them. It's their job to write about things they don't like.

   TIM: You may be right. But now I'm interested in seeing the show. I'll be right back. I'm going to get us a *snack* to eat while we're watching. Who knows? Maybe I'll become a **fan,** like you.

5. **fan** means:
   a. person who likes a certain movie, TV show, or famous person
   b. TV actor
   c. person who writes the scripts for TV shows

The Life of an Actor

You or your partner should read the following story. Use the other words in the sentence to help you understand the boldface words.

I really enjoy being an actor. Right now, I'm acting in a play. I've been in a movie before. I played a small part in *Star Trek IV* (the **sequel** to *Star Trek III*). But acting on the **stage** is entirely different from acting in a movie. If you make a mistake, there's no chance to do anything over again.

The night the play opened, we were afraid no one would come. But by 7:00 P.M. there were already about twenty-five people standing in line outside the **box office** waiting to be **admitted** to the theater.

As I was putting my *costume* on, I felt nervous. I was worried that I would forget my lines. But when the play began, I remembered everything. The only thing that went wrong was that in the first **scene** a vase fell down and broke. I had to act like this event was planned.

When the play was over, the **audience** seemed to have liked our **performance.** I would have felt terrible if anyone had **booed!** But they **applauded** loudly for a long time. The stage assistant must have gotten tired of opening and closing the curtain while we bowed. We got eleven **curtain calls!**

If you don't understand the meaning of the boldface words, review their definitions at the beginning of this chapter.

With your partner, use the words beneath each picture to describe it.

box office

sequel

scene

to be admitted

performance

curtain call

to applaud

to boo

stage

audience

CONVERSATION
TV in Other Countries

Follow along as the teacher reads the examples and the questions formed from them. Ask the teacher for more examples if you do not understand how to form the questions.

Example 1: Find the country in which people have the greatest number of TV's in their homes.

Question: How many TV's do people in your country have in their homes?

Example 2: Find the country where there are the most TV **commercials.**

Question: About how many TV **commercials** are there in an hour in your country?

*When your teacher assigns you **one** of the following directions, make it into a question. Then, walk around the room and ask the other students your question. When you think that you have found the country that your direction asks for, write it on the line beneath your direction.*

1. Find the country where foreign TV shows are the most popular.

_____

_____

2. Find the country in which people spend the most time watching TV.

_____

_____

3. Find the country that has the most TV **channels.**

_____

_____

4. Find the country in which there is the most **censorship** on TV.

_____

_____

5. Find the country in which there is the least freedom about the things that can be advertised in TV **commercials.**

_____

_____

6. Find the country in which parents are the most *strict* about what their children watch on TV.

_____

_____

7. Find the country in which there is the most international news on TV.

_____

_____

8. Find the country that has had TV for the longest time.

_____

_____

Tell the class what country you have found and why you chose it as your answer.

Making a Movie

Part 1. *You and your group are moviemakers. Look at the example pictures from a "movie." Listen as your teacher reads what happens in each* **scene.**

Example Pictures

Part 2. *Look at the set of pictures that the teacher assigns your group. You have filmed these "shots" to make a movie. Together, begin putting the pictures in order so that they tell a story. Talk about what happens in each picture, and write the story on the lines next to it. (You may put the pictures in any order, but you must use all of them in your film.)*

Set A

1.

2.

_____
_____
_____
_____
_____
_____
_____

3.

_____
_____
_____
_____
_____
_____
_____

4.

_____
_____
_____
_____
_____
_____
_____

5.

_____
_____
_____
_____
_____
_____
_____

Set B

1.

_____
_____
_____
_____
_____
_____
_____

2.

_____
_____
_____
_____
_____
_____

3.

_____
_____
_____
_____
_____
_____
_____

4.

_____
_____
_____
_____
_____
_____

5.

_____

_____

_____

_____

_____

_____

Have the members of your group take turns presenting the **scenes** *of your movie to the class.*

Entertainment around the World

What is entertainment like in your country? With the other members of your group, take turns reading the following questions. After each question is read, every group member should answer about his or her country.

1. What kinds of entertainers *are* most *respected* in your country? (For example, are movie actors more *respected* than TV actors?)

2. When a famous person is seen in a public place, what kinds of things do his or her **fans** do?

3. How do people **applaud** when they like a **performance?** Do actors on **stage** sometimes receive **curtain calls?**

4. How do people **boo** when they don't like a performance?

5. What kinds of things might an **audience** in a theater do that would be considered bad *etiquette*?

6. Do you have **critics** who write **reviews** for movies, plays, or TV **series?** Where do their **reviews** appear?

7. Do some of the movies made in your country have **sequels?** If so, what kinds of movies have them?

8. Are there some kinds of movies that children or teenagers can't get **admitted** to? What kinds of movies are they? Are there some kinds of movies that aren't shown in your country? What kinds are they?

9. Must you go to a **box office** to buy tickets for movies, plays, and sports events, or can you buy them at other places? (For example, in the United States, tickets for these events are sometimes sold in certain stores or on college campuses.)

10. Do you have **cable TV** in your country? What kinds of things can you see on **cable TV** that you can't see on other **channels?**

11. Do you have **TV listings** in your country? If so, where can you find them?

12. How are TV **ratings** decided in your country? (For example, in the United States, a special machine is attached to the TV sets of certain families. The

machines record how often each TV show is watched. Then, the people who are taking the **ratings** collect the machines and add up the totals for each show.)

Tell the class something that you learned about another country from a group member.

Writing a TV Commercial

You work for an advertising agency. With your coworkers, choose one of the following subjects, and make up a TV **commercial** *about it.*

      a car

      jeans

      a soft drink

      a movie

      a laundry soap

      a radio, stereo, or TV

      a shampoo

      a place to go for entertainment (such as Disneyland)

      a *dating service*

      (If you do not like any of these topics, you and your coworkers may choose one of your own.)

Use the following questions to help you.

1. What is the name of the thing that you will be advertising?
2. What can it do for a person?
3. Why should a person buy it or spend money for it?

Practice your **commercial** *and present it to the class.*

When the Lights Went Out (A Play)

Choose one member of your group to read the introduction to the play. After the introduction is read, decide which group members will be Jane, Tom, Susan, and Mike. When it is your turn, read your lines. Together, complete the dialogue.

Introduction to the play: Four friends are traveling through Europe together. In the evening they stop at a mysterious old hotel in the country. They are eating dinner in the hotel dining room when the play begins.

JANE:	This sure is a nice old hotel!
TOM:	It sure is! I never thought we'd find such nice *accommodations*!
SUSAN:	I think it's kind of scary here myself. But I'm *thankful* we got here before the storm began.
MIKE:	I know. It's really raining hard outside now.
TOM:	What's happening? Who turned out the lights?
SUSAN:	The electricity must have gone out because of the storm.
JANE:	Oh, good! Someone's lighting some lamps.
TOM:	Hey, where's Mike?
JANE:	I don't know. But I'm worried about him. He's been acting strangely for the last few days.
SUSAN:	Look! The window's open.
TOM:	Yeah! And what's that light moving away from the hotel?

: _____
_____

: _____
_____

: _____
_____

: _____
_____

: _____
_____

: _____
_____

: _____
_____

: _____
_____

: _____
_____

Practice the whole play and present it to the class.

CHAPTER
10 The World

VOCABULARY

Study the following vocabulary.

Nouns

charity – organization that gives money to people who need it

contribution – gift of money or help to someone

the environment – the air, water, and land around us

famine – condition in which people in a certain part of the world don't have enough food

greed – desire for very great amounts of money or property without care for other people

humanity – the human race; human beings; all the people who live on Earth

overpopulation – the condition of having too many people in a place

poverty – the condition of being poor

progress – movement toward becoming more modern

space – area that has nothing in it

technology – the use of science to make the world more modern

wealth – lots of money or valuable property

Verbs

to adapt – to change in order to be comfortable in a new situation

to aid – to help

to devastate – to destroy or ruin

to pollute – to make (the air, water, or earth) unclean

Adjectives

global – worldwide; throughout the world; over the entire earth

ideal – perfect

rural – country; having to do with the country

urban – having to do with the city

Please Make a Contribution

With your partner, take turns reading lines of the following dialogue. Choose the correct vocabulary word to put into each blank.

(Yoshi comes out of the grocery store. Suddenly a young woman comes up to him.)

ELLEN: Excuse me. Would you like to make a _____ ?

YOSHI: To what? Are you representing a _____ , or something?

ELLEN: Yes. We're the Public Assistance League. We

_____ poor people throughout the United States by helping them buy food and clothing.

YOSHI: Surely, there aren't that many people living in

_____ in this country, except in a few big cities.

ELLEN: That's not quite true. There are a lot of people in big cities who are hungry and who don't even have a place to live, but there are also

many people in _____ areas who don't have enough to eat.

rural – country; having to do with the country

aid – help

charity – organization that gives money to people who need it

contribution – gift of money or help to someone

poverty – the condition of being poor

A Frightening Situation

Cover the left-hand side of the page with a piece of paper. Then, listen as your teacher reads the dialogue. After each section is read, choose the best definition for the boldface word.

(*Susan and Mike are driving to work together in Mike's car. They begin talking about the news.*)

1. SUSAN: I heard on the news that the ocean is twice as dirty as it was a few years ago.

    MIKE: That's upsetting. It's frightening to see the **environment** being destroyed.

1. **environment** means:
   a. air, water, and land that are around us
   b. works of art
   c. government

2. SUSAN: I've never understood why some people would want to destroy it.

    MIKE: Well, it's because of their **greed.** All they care about is getting richer and richer.

2. **greed** means:
   a. desire for as much money as is necessary
   b. desire for more money or property than is necessary
   c. unkindness

3. SUSAN: I know that, but how will money help them if they ruin the world we live in?

    MIKE: I guess people like that think that if they get enough **wealth** they can go live somewhere where they won't be *affected* by what they do.

3. **wealth** means:
   a. friends
   b. money
   c. knowledge

4. SUSAN: That's a silly idea! We all share the same oceans and the same air. We're all hurt when bad things happen to the earth.

    MIKE: We understand that, but some people don't, so they just go on **devastating** the environment.

4. **devastating** means:
   a. helping
   b. cleaning up
   c. destroying

5. SUSAN: There must be something we can do to stop them.

    MIKE: You know, one thing we can do is become members of an organization that's fighting to protect the environment. Maybe we can't build an **ideal** world, but we can make a better one.

5. **ideal** means:
   a. larger
   b. more crowded
   c. perfect

Some Problems that We Share

You or your partner should read the following story. Use the other words in the sentence to help you understand the boldface words.

Until recently, almost everyone thought that growth and **progress** would make the world a better place. They believed that something new was always better than something old.

So countries have spent billions of dollars on science and engineering to develop new ways of making things and doing work. Now some people believe that this new **technology** is the main cause of the world's problems. One such problem has come from the invention of the car. In some crowded **urban** areas, the car has **polluted** the air so badly that people get sick just from breathing it. Waste from nuclear power plants is another example of how technology is harming the earth. When nuclear waste is put into the seas, it can hurt or kill animals and fish.

Other people feel that the main reason for the world's difficulties is **overpopulation**. They think that the growing number of people is the cause of **famines.** Famines result when a country has too many people to feed, or when it sells too much food to another country that does not have enough food for its own people. Overpopulation also causes a lack of **space**. And it is difficult for **humanity** to **adapt** to living in smaller areas.

There is a lot of argument on this subject. But almost everyone agrees on one thing. We must do something quickly. When the problems get worse, they will not *affect* just a few countries. They will be **global** problems that *affect* us all.

If you don't understand the meaning of the boldface words, review their definitions at the beginning of this chapter.

With your partner, use the words beneath each picture to describe it.

progress

urban

to adapt

technology

to pollute

global
overpopulation
famine
humanity
space

CONVERSATION
Who Would You Be?

You are a person who has had a great influence on the world. (You may be a real person or a person whom you make up.) Your partner is a reporter for the newspaper, "The Daily Planet." Listen as your teacher reads the example. Then, tell your partner about yourself when he or she asks you the following questions.

1. Who are you?
2. What *significant* **contribution** have you made to the world?
3. Where do you live and work? Why have you chosen to live and work there?
4. How is your life different from other people's lives?
5. What kinds of people do you know?

Reverse roles.

Tell the class who your partner would be.

What's Happening in 2030?

It is the year 2030. You and your group work for a TV news show. Together, make up a news program that tells about what the world is like. Include the following:

1. World news—for example, how there is no longer enough **space** on earth for people to live, so some of them are being sent to other planets.

2. Local news—for example, how psychologists at a nearby university have made a discovery that will be important for all **humanity:** they have found the secret of happiness.

3. A *commercial* for a new product—for example, a car that is driven by a computer.

4. An editorial (that tells what people should do about a certain problem)—for example, a company has invented a new drug that will help people live to be 300 years old. But, because of **greed,** the company is asking a high price for the drug so only people with great **wealth** can buy it. The company should lower the price, so that everyone can afford it.

5. A humorous story—for example, a robot that was working in the home of some wealthy people is no longer employed tonight. When the guests for a dinner party arrived, the robot accidentally served food that had been meant for the owner's dog.

Practice the news program and present it to the class.

A House in the Country

*How does **progress** change people's lives? With the other members of your group, make up a story about the following pictures. Use the questions to help you.*

Look at the picture.

1. Is the house in the picture in a **rural** or **urban** area? Why do you think so?

2. Make up a description of the people who live in the house. Who are they? How old are they? What do they do? What are their interests or *goals*?

3. What kinds of work do the neighbors of these people do?

Look at the picture. Answer the following questions about it.

1. What changes have taken place because of **technology** since the last picture?

2. How well have the people who live in the house **adapted** to these changes? (How have the changes made their lives better or worse?)

Look at the pictures. Answer the last set of questions for each of the pictures.

Tell the class the story that you have made up about the pictures.

Designing an Ideal Country

*Design an **ideal** country. With the other members of your group, take turns reading the following questions. After each question is read, every group member should answer. Together, agree on the best answer(s) for each question.*

1. What is the weather like? (For example, how hot or cold is it? Does it rain or snow a lot?)

2. What kinds of things do people in your country do to stay healthy? (For example, what kinds of exercise do they do? What do they eat and drink?)

3. What is the educational system like? (For example, is anything done to make sure that all people can go to school if they want to? Is there anything special about the schools here?)

4. What is the work situation like? (For example, how much do people work? What special things do companies have or do to make their employees happy?)

5. How do people behave toward each other? (For example, in what ways do people help each other? What special **charities** does your country have?)

6. How does your country help to solve social problems such as **overpopulation, poverty,** and crime?

7. What does the government do to protect the **environment** and wildlife? (Are *penalties* given to companies that **pollute** the water and air? What kind of *penalties*? What kind of *penalties* are given to people who kill wild animals illegally?)

8. How does your country **aid** other countries that have been **devastated** by earthquakes or floods? What kinds of **global** problems (for example, **famine**, disease) does your country help solve?

*Tell the class about the **ideal** country that you have designed.*

Wishes for the World

What wishes would you make for the world? With the other members of your group, look at the following topics. By yourself, choose a wish that you would make for each topic. Tell your choices and your reasons for choosing them to the group. Together, try to agree on the best wish for each topic.

1. **the environment** (for example, that every country could have clean air) _____

   _____

2. **medicine** (for example, a cure for cancer) _____

   _____

3. **relations between countries** (for example, that countries would stop making

   nuclear weapons) _____

   _____

4. **people's values and ways of thinking** (for example, that people all over the

   world would learn to be more cooperative, and less *competitive*) _____

   _____

5. **basic human needs** (for example, that everyone in the world could have a

   comfortable place to live) _____

   _____

   _____

6. **other** _____

   _____

Tell the class some of the wishes that you have made for the world.